STO

DO NOT REMOVE
CARDS FROM POCKET

1-9-95

THEY WROTE THEIR OWN HEADLINES:
American Women Journalists

World Writers

THEY WROTE THEIR OWN HEADLINES:
American Women Journalists

Nancy Whitelaw

MORGAN
REYNOLDS
Incorporated

Greensboro

THEY WROTE THEIR OWN HEADLINES:
American Women Journalists

Library of Congress Cataloging-in-Publication Data
Whitelaw, Nancy.
  They wrote their own headlines : American women journalists / Nancy Whitelaw.
      p.   cm. -- (World writers)
  Includes bibliographical references and index.
  ISBN 1-883846-06-4
  1. Women journalists—United States—Biography—Juvenile literature. [1. Journalists.
2. Women—Biography.]   I. Title. II. Series.
PN4872.W45 1994
070' .92273 -- dc20

                                                        93-50818
                                                           CIP
                                                            AC

Printed in the United States of America

First Edition

*Dedicated with love and thanks to
Pat Brininger and Carolyn Seymour*

CONTENTS

Ida Tarbell (Library of Congress)

Ida M. Tarbell, investigative reporter, uncovered evidence of corruption, bribery, and illegal price-setting by the Standard Oil Company. Colleagues and friends feared for her life. "They will get you in the end," they warned. "Don't do it," begged her father. Ida refused to let fear control her career. Her series of articles resulted in a Supreme Court decision against the Standard Oil Company.

IDA M. TARBELL— ACTIVIST

1857 - 1944

Ida Tarbell grew up in the mid-1800s in Pennsylvania oil country, near the town of Titusville, where her father was a small oil producer and speculator. She breathed the bitter smell of oil everywhere. The greasy liquid coated trees and shrubs, and seeped into skin and clothes and buildings. Open pits of oil stood on all sides. Great streams of oil, called "gushers," rose straight into the air, sometimes as high as two hundred feet. Wooden oil derricks stood in the Tarbell's front yard. Ida and her friends played on them when their parents weren't watching.

Most of the time, Ida obeyed her parents, was a good student, and enjoyed her friends. But when she had to go to a new school at the age of thirteen, Ida rebelled. She didn't like being a "new" kid or having different teachers. So she skipped school a few times. Nobody seemed to notice. She skipped more and more often, enjoying every minute she spent wandering in fields and woods. She created collections of pebbles and rocks, gathered leaves, and studied insects. She marveled at the beauty of beads of water on a leaf, or the careful construction of a bird's nest.

One day her teacher took her aside and scolded her harshly. How could a bright student like Ida waste her intelligence? Ida was startled. Like a flash, she understood that she alone was responsible for her life. Within a few months, she became a model student.

Most of all, Ida loved science classes. She studied zoology, chemistry, and botany. She learned to identify and classify objects that intrigued her. Her microscope brought new worlds to her. She explored hangnails, fly wings, buttercup petals—anything else that would fit on the slide.

While Ida busied herself with nature, the community around her busied itself with oil. The discovery of oil in Titusville brought hundreds of jobs in drilling, producing, and marketing as well as hundreds more in the furnishing of food, clothing, and shelter for the oil workers. It was a prosperous, but noisy, overcrowded, and dirty town.

Titusville oil was sent by railroad to Cleveland, Pittsburgh, and other larger cities. Suddenly, local producers learned that their rail rates would double. Worse, these rates would decrease for the South Improvement Company, a competitor who sold to the same markets as the Titusville companies.

The Tarbells, their neighbors, and most people connected with Titusville oil suspected the cause of the doubled rail rates was John D. Rockefeller, the wealthy president of the Standard Oil Company. They heard rumors that he wanted to squeeze small oil producers out of the market. People were saying that he had created the South Improvement Company and then bribed the railroads to manipulate freight costs. His next move would be to buy out the smaller companies, once they were weakened by unfair competition.

The people of Titusville demonstrated with impassioned speeches, raids on oil cars, and appeals to the state legislature and to the U. S. Congress. The railroads were forced to cancel the freight increases. Despite the victory, Ida never forgot the powerful threat of Rockefeller's money and status. She wrote later: "There was born in me a hatred of privilege—privilege of any sort."

Of course, this did not signal the end of privilege for wealthy and powerful people. Soon the residents of Titusville found themselves fighting against Rockefeller again. The millionaire failed to honor an agreement to buy their oil, and the small producers were unable to force him to keep his side of the bargain.

Until then, Ida had believed that hard work and determination guaranteed success. After that, she understood that outside forces could destroy all that hard work had built.

Like most girls in those days, Ida had no real career plans. She knew only that she did not want to get married. She did not want to live as her mother did, with no say in family finances. When her father thought that her mother spent too much money, he scolded her. Without any budget guidelines, Ida's mother could only accept the scolding and spend less. Ida assumed that all husband-wife relationships were like this. At night she prayed that God would spare her from marriage.

An unmarried woman needed a career. Ida decided to become a teacher, and at age 19, entered Allegheny College in Meadville, Pennsylvania. Ida was slim and almost six feet tall, with long dark hair. Like her fellow students, she wore a fashionable, tightly-fitted, long black dress to class. In her calisthenics class, she wore the required "bloomers" and high-necked blouses.

All the courses interested her—English literature, literary criticism, science, French, and German. But again, science was her favorite subject. She became editor of a college publication and was active in a literary society.

After graduation in 1880, Ida became a teacher in the small town of Poland, Ohio. Her very heavy teaching load included classes in Greek, Latin, French, German, geology, botany, geometry, and trigonometry. Most of the students were trained only to memorize, not to learn. After two difficult years, Ida admitted that she found little satisfaction in teaching.

Ida had fleeting thoughts about pursuing her interests in

science, perhaps as a naturalist. But this career choice was not open to women. She remained true to her vow to stay single. She declared, "I never met a man I would want always at my side night and day, and I am sure I will not." In 1882, she returned to Titusville with no clear plans for the future.

A part-time job opened up for her, editing a literary magazine, *The Chautauquan.* Gradually, Ida took duties beyond editing. She worked on a few articles, learned how to prepare the magazine for printing, and answered letters to the editor. She began to see writing as a possible career.

Ida tried writing short stories. Despite her enthusiasm at the start, she lacked the inspiration to finish them. Her next career consideration was journalism. Her editor at *The Chautauquan* was not ready to accept a woman journalist. He told her flatly that she had been hired to edit, not to write.

Thirty-three-year-old Ida needed more challenge and more independence. If she could not advance her career where she was, then she would move. Her plans grew as she realized that she could be independent if she dared to try.

Ida's plans included living in France where she would write articles and send them back to America. She also wanted to write a biography of Madame Manon Roland, a French martyr she admired.

When she told newspaper editors of her plans, a few agreed to consider articles she submitted from France. Some editors refused, like the one who said, "You're not a writer. You'll starve."

In 1891, after a few months' study of conversational French, Ida and two women friends sailed to Paris. Ida went with great expectations for her new life, but with only $150.00 in cash.

Paris was exciting with its new Eiffel Tower, electric street lights, and the mixed crowds of artists, wealthy socialites, beggars, and tourists. Ida wrote dozens of articles—sketches of the people she met, reflections on attitudes toward women, reports on working conditions for women, and descriptions of the city. To get to know the people, she worked in a soup kitchen and made friends with students in the Latin Quarter. From the Moulin Rouge, a famous nightclub, she wrote articles about the dancers who performed the controversial "can-can." American editors in Pittsburgh, Cincinnati, and Chicago eagerly bought her articles. She was thrilled to receive $5.00 for each one.

Ida also worked on her biography of Madame Roland,

and wrote a romantic short story, "France Adoree." She was stunned with delight when the popular *Scribners' Magazine* sent her $100 for the piece.

Samuel McClure, editor of the well-liked *McClure's Magazine*, gave her a steady job as a free-lancer from Paris. She interviewed the great scientist Louis Pasteur, wrote about criminal investigation procedures, and other diverse subjects. Once, as she took notes on a student demonstration, she barely escaped a rain of bullets. She did research in food safety. Ida never ran out of ideas for articles.

In 1894, Ida returned to Titusville for a visit. She learned that John D. Rockefeller was still driving independent oil producers out of business. Government officials could not, or would not, stop him. Ida's father and brother were both losing money on their oil leases.

Ida could not help her family financially. Nor could she stay in Titusville, a place where she had no future. She accepted a job in New York as a full-time writer for *McClure's*. Her first assignment was overwhelming: to write a biography of Napoleon Bonaparte, with the first installment due in only three months. Ida worked six days a week on the research and writing. Because it kept her so busy, she called it "biography on the gallop." She wrote with flowing style, and simple language. Her research materials included reminiscences, letters, anecdotes, and books. The magazine series became a huge success.

After publication in the magazine, the collection of articles became a best-selling book, *A Short Life of Napoleon Bonaparte*. Because Ida's name had become well-known, the Scribners' publishing company agreed to publish her biography of Madame Roland.

For her next assignment, McClure asked Ida to edit some papers about President Lincoln, assassinated some thirty years before. She discovered more than 300 letters and speeches that had never been used as sources, and collected other anecdotes. She wrote of Lincoln's conversations with storekeepers, his informal meetings with soldiers during the Civil War, and his ideas about religion. The series of Lincoln articles ran for a year, and brought new subscribers to *McClure's*. She followed this with another series, focusing on a later period in Lincoln's life.

Although by now she was one of the most popular writers in America, Ida remained unmoved by fame. An interviewer wrote about her: "She has no pride in her success. She plods persistently through any task, meeting every new emergency with a new resource and when finished puts it aside ..."

In 1899, Ida became the temporary managing editor of *McClure's*. Under her guidance, the magazine published stories by humorist Mark Twain and by Rudyard Kipling, famed author of tales about India. She also helped Ray Stannard Baker, a reporter who often wrote about workers' conditions and rights. Under Ida Tarbell, *McClure's* encouraged a sense of social responsibility in each citizen. One editor at the magazine described Ida "as firm as the Statue of Liberty, and holding up the lantern of integrity ... her concern was honest information."

By 1900, the American economy was growing. Much political discussion focused on "trusts," the mergers of smaller companies into one great company. Trusts existed in many industries, including oil, sugar, steel, and beef.

Economists and politicians debated about trusts. Some citizens believed that larger companies helped keep consumer prices down by the efficient use of resources. Others thought that huge companies raised prices by limiting competition.

Ida decided to bring the debate to the pages of *McClure's*. John D. Rockefeller's trust, the Standard Oil Company, was well-known. She would write a history of this trust. Then readers could decide whether they thought the trust served the citizens or just the officials of Standard Oil.

Ida still had bitter memories of the South Improvement Company. Although Rockefeller denied any connection with the firm, Ida was skeptical. However, she imposed on herself the responsibility of writing the series with fairness and honesty.

Ida had problems from her first attempts at research. Important Standard Oil papers were missing; highly placed officials refused to talk to her. Franklin Tarbell warned his daughter not to write the piece. "Don't do it, Ida," he said. "They [Standard Oil] will ruin the magazine." An official in the Rockefeller-controlled National City Bank told her that he was concerned about her research. "Well, I am sorry," she answered, "but of course that makes no difference to me."

Ida spent two years interviewing, reading, collecting and checking information, and writing the history. Editors at *McClure's* scrutinized each article three times. Each time they sent the manuscript back to Ida, who re-worked the material without complaint. A literary editor at the office said the other editors "pounded her and her stuff to make the best of it page by page."

In 1902, *McClure's* published the first article of the series. Ida began by describing the discovery of oil in Pennsylvania and the large numbers of people who became involved in the industry. She depicted hard-working, honest people earning a good life in the oil industry. Her memory served her well in writing about how the Titusville citizens reacted to the rise in railroad rates.

Rockefeller had said publicly that he had nothing to do with the formation of the South Improvement Company. Ida disagreed. She quoted from reports of a Congressional investigation committee. A witness at the investigation testified that he was present when Rockefeller purchased the South Improvement Company. The witness, like everyone else present, had yielded to Rockefeller's demand for complete secrecy. To further prove her point, Ida showed photos of Rockefeller attending South Improvement Company meetings. She described the company as "a big hand [that] reached out from nobody knew where, to steal their conquest and throttle their future."

Luckily, the articles brought no threats to Ida's career or her life. She commented, "... now that the thing is well under way, and I have not been kidnapped or sued for libel ..., people are willing to talk freely to me."

Ida's work was noticed—unfavorably—by President Theodore Roosevelt. For journalists like Ida, President Roosevelt invented the term 'muckraker.' He meant writers who dig around in muck and dirt, making trouble, but not solving problems. However, he did order further investigation of trusts.

Ida got a lucky break when a Standard Oil worker discovered incriminating evidence in office waste baskets. Some of the records in the baskets referred to spying by Standard Oil on smaller companies. Ida was sickened by this evidence. "There was a littleness about it that seemed utterly contemptible," she reported.

In 1904, the complete series of popular articles was published in two volumes, *The History of Standard Oil*. A reviewer wrote that the history was "the most remarkable book of its kind ever written in this country." McClure told Ida, "You are today the most generally famous woman in America."

Although she may have been a famous woman, Ida was not recognized everywhere as a journalist. For example, the prestigious Periodical Publishers' group did not invite her to a dinner for leading writers. Guests included publisher Sam McClure, activist Ray Baker, journalist Lincoln Steffens, and other males, but not Ida. She complained, "It is the first time since I came into the office that the fact of petticoats has stood in my way."

Despite that snub, Ida had a rich social life. One reporter noted, "It is doubtful whether any other woman in New York is welcomed in so many or so varied social circles as she."

In November 1906, the U. S. Attorney General charged Standard Oil with conspiring to control interstate commerce in oil. Standard Oil lost that case, and finally, in May 1911, the Supreme Court upheld the conviction. The Standard Oil trust was finally broken.

Next, Ida wrote a seven-part history of feminism in the United States. In one article, she said that women did not need to vote. They could exert their power by the way they brought up their children, she believed. In "Man's Inhumanity to Women," she expressed sympathy for the shopgirls in the garment business who fought for better working conditions. She urged women to fight for a maximum ten-hour working day.

As research for her writing, she became a worker in a fabric mill in Rhode Island. She spent hours with "shrieking

spinning machines and the banging looms," in temperatures
of ninety degrees and higher. She reported: "After ten hours
at spindle or loom the woman hurries to a cold, unkempt
house, which she must make comfortable and cheerful if
it is to be so ..."

At age 58, Ida branched out into new markets. She wrote
for *Woman's Home Companion* and other popular magazines. She wrote her only novel, *The Rising of the Tide: The
Story of Sabinsport*, about the attitudes of small-town
citizens toward the coming of a war.

She accepted an assignment to give a series of speeches
in Ohio and Pennsylvania on "The Ideals of Business." Ida
enjoyed talking before crowds, and she liked traveling.

In 1918, doctors found that Ida was suffering from
Parkinson's disease, a progressive palsy for which there was
no treatment. Though ill, Ida continued to write as much
as she was able.

Ida wanted to survey the international scene again. In
January 1919, she traveled to Europe. Her assignment was
to write articles for *Red Cross Magazine* about life in Europe
at the end of World War I. She sent back articles about the
tremendous devastation—whole families wiped out, build-

ings obliterated, the lack of necessities such as food, clothing, and shelter.

Ida could not get the horror of war out of her mind. In
1921, she covered a conference on arms limitation. She
collected her articles in a book titled *Peacemakers—Blessed
and Otherwise*.

The reporter traveled to Italy in 1926, on an assignment
from *McCall's*. She was to write a four-part series on Benito
Mussolini, the dictator of Italy. Sixty-nine-year-old Ida
refused to listen to friends and fellow correspondents who
warned about the leader's prejudice against Americans, and
of his brutal military police. But Ida traveled safely, and
returned with exciting and perceptive articles.

In later years, Parkinson's disease restricted Ida severely.
In 1928, friends noted that she was slight, frail, and tired-
looking. However, she agreed to write her autobiography,
All in a Day's Work. She learned to use a typewriter; her
hands were too shaky to use a pencil anymore. When typing
became difficult, she dictated to a secretary. In public, she
sat on her hands rather than allow people to see how much
they trembled. Her legs jerked with each step, pitching her
forward awkwardly.

On her eightieth birthday in 1937, Ida received so many affectionate cards that she and her secretary spent two days just opening them. She started a book, *Life after Eighty*, but could not finish it.

On January 6, 1944, Ida Tarbell died of pneumonia in a Connecticut hospital. As she requested, her body was buried in Titusville.

Today, Ida Minerva Tarbell is remembered as the "little lady who beat Standard Oil." But she never took credit for her success. In her autobiography, she wrote:

> "I have never had illusions about the value of my individual contribution! I realized early that what a man or a woman does is built on what those who have gone before have done, that its real value depends on making the matter a little clearer, a little sounder for those who come after. Nobody begins or ends anything. Each person is a link, weak or strong, in an endless chain."

IDA TARBELL'S BOOKS

A Short Life of Napoleon Bonaparte

The Early Life of Abraham Lincoln, with J. McCan Davis

Madame Roland: A Biographical Study

The Life of Abraham Lincoln, 2 vols.

Napoleon's Addresses

History of the Standard Oil Company

A Souvenir of Lincoln's Birthday, Feb. 12, 1907, with F.T.
   Hill and R. L. Jones

He Knew Lincoln

Father Abraham

*Selections from the Letters, Speeches, and State Papers of
   Abraham Lincoln*

The Tariff in Our Times

The Business of Being a Woman

Ways of Woman

New Ideals in Business

The Rising of the Tide: The Story of Sabinsport

In Lincoln's Chair

Boy Scout's Life of Lincoln

He Knew Lincoln, and Other Billy Brown Stories

Peacemakers—Blessed and Otherwise

In the Footsteps of the Lincolns

Life of Elbert H. Gary

A Reporter for Lincoln: Story of Henry E. Wing, Soldier and Newspaper Man

Owen D. Young: A New Type of Industrial Leader

The Nationalizing of Business, 1878-1898

Women at Work: A Tour Among Careers

All in the Day's Work: An Autobiography

Dorothy Thompson (Library of Congress)

Time *magazine called Dorothy Thompson a model for American women: "...emancipated, articulate, and successful, living in the thick of one of the most exciting periods of history and interpreting it to millions."*

DOROTHY THOMPSON— FOREIGN CORRESPONDENT
1893 - 1961

Even as a child, Dorothy Thompson was ready for adventure. When she was three years old, she set out along the Erie Railroad tracks in upstate New York. When her parents found her, she told them that she was trying to find the world.

Later, Dorothy spent a lot of time on the railroad bridges, dreaming about the day when she would ride on one of those railroad cars that rumbled by. Once she threw her straw hat on top of a passing freight car, just for the fun of watching it glide away.

She could create her own adventure. Tramping to school on a snowy day in Buffalo, New York, she would dream that she was in a vast Siberia-like land. All the way to school, she was on the alert against howling wolves, frostbite, and starvation.

In summer, sturdy Dorothy Thompson would push her short brown braids back impatiently. In a wink, she became tall, slim, black-haired Dorothy, strolling in an exotic garden, enchanting her audience, who gazed at her in awe.

When a tornado damaged their neighborhood, seven-year-old Dorothy watched as her parents cared for fearful and injured friends. In her waking dreams, she became a nurse, caring for injured soldiers.

Dorothy became a part of the real world as she made parish calls with her father, who was a minister. From him, she learned to talk with people in all walks of life. She visited in fancy homes ornate with towers, stained-glass windows, and long porches. She met women dressed in the latest fashion of the day—ankle-length dresses and hair-dos piled high on their heads. She also visited in neighborhoods where much smaller houses were black with soot and smoke from the Lackawanna steel mills. There she met women wearing tattered dresses, many of them holding ragged children.

When Dorothy was only eight years old, her mother died. At first, she reacted only with shock. Beloved Aunt Lizzie, a widow with ten grown children, tried to take the mother's place in the Thompson family. Dorothy received some comfort from her. She also enlarged her dream world by reading everything she could find, whether she understood it or not. She tackled Charles Dickens' English novels, William Shakespeare's sixteenth-century plays, the Bible, and popular novels she found in the local library.

Teachers knew Dorothy as the mischievous student who rigged up a string to activate a tin can noise-maker in a fellow student's desk. She was the one who usually had her hand up in class, and who argued with teachers. Neighbors knew her as a mischief-maker who made moonlight raids on melon patches, created a cemetery for cats, locked the janitor in the church basement, and crawled under church pews after Sunday services to look for dropped coins. Her family knew her as an ever-active youngster, ice skating, jumping about in hay lofts, riding horses bareback, and sliding down hills on bobsleds. Dorothy wrote in her autobiography: "I can hardly remember myself between the ages of nine and twelve without a bandage or a scab."

In 1912, Dorothy enrolled in Syracuse University in New

York state. Unlike most of her friends, she didn't want to be a wife and mother. She wanted a career, one involved with helping less fortunate people.

Dorothy loved the social life at Syracuse, replete with games and parties. She was also an excellent student. Because she loved reading, Dorothy tried writing. She submitted some short stories to magazines. When they were rejected, though, she assumed she had no talent for writing.

After graduation in 1914, Dorothy worked for an advertising company. She left after six months because, she said, "I could not see that I was contributing anything either to my own development or to the society in which I lived."

Next, Dorothy worked for the New York State Women's Suffrage Party, an organization created to lobby for women's right to vote. Her job was to persuade local officials to let her give speeches, during which she asked for contributions. Dorothy was a dramatic as well as a persuasive talker. One woman said that she gave a contribution because she enjoyed the "show" that Dorothy put on. To her surprise, she earned praise for her speeches, and later for her written commentaries. She gained back some confidence in her ability to write. This confidence increased when some of her articles were published in New York newspapers, such as the *Sun*, the *Times*, and the *Tribune*. Soon, she was on her way to becoming a journalist.

In 1920, 27-year-old Dorothy dreamed of becoming an international reporter. She had always wanted to travel, and Europe seemed an exciting place. The First World War had ended, leaving a continent faced with the re-building of a war-torn society, and hopefully of creating a lasting peace. She asked several newspaper editors to sponsor her trip, promising to send back articles with wide reader appeal. When no editors accepted her proposal, she managed to scrape together enough money on her own to make the trip.

Dorothy did research for her first international story on the twelve-day trip across the Atlantic Ocean; she spent hours informally interviewing some of her fellow passengers. These were Jews active in the Zionist movement, which was an effort to establish a Jewish homeland. They were on their way to an international Zionist conference, and were eager to explain their lives, their beliefs, and their dreams to the young reporter.

From London, Dorothy sold an article on Zionism to the International News Services. This syndicate distributed articles to newspapers all over the United States.

Dorothy moved on to freelancing, sending unsolicited manuscripts to newspapers like *The Christian Science Monitor* and popular magazines like *Outlook*. Most of her articles were about people and life in Europe, and had a charming combination of facts, shrewd perceptions, and good humor. Many of her articles were accepted. The name of Dorothy Thompson was becoming familiar among editors, readers, and other journalists.

She made the most of a lucky break when she happened to meet a leader of a rebellion in Ireland. She interviewed Terence MacSwiney, Lord Mayor of Cork. One hour after their interview, he was jailed for treason. His story became internationally important when he died two months later, after a self-imposed hunger strike. The International News Service published the story, and rewarded her with an assignment in Austria.

Dorothy wrote about the many aspects of Austrian life which enchanted her, such as the elaborate funerals, the strong coffee, the sour wine, the easygoing people, and popular Austrian love songs.

Dorothy was creative about getting stories. To interview the exiled emperor and the pregnant empress of Hungary, she put on a Red Cross nurse's uniform as a disguise. She was admitted to the heavily guarded castle where the royal couple was staying; she convinced the guards she had come to help the Empress. When the story hit the papers, correspondents everywhere admired—and envied—journalist Dorothy Thompson.

She filled both day and night with dinners, parties, nightclubs, informal gatherings, and formal meetings. Always, she was searching for a story. She had advice for young women who wanted to be journalists: "Don't accept for an instant the theory that it's a man's job, and don't be flattered by the phrase, 'You write like a man.'"

Dorothy and Joseph Bard, a writer and lawyer, fell in love in Hungary. They married in Budapest in 1923.

The couple moved to Berlin in 1925 when Dorothy became bureau chief for the *Public Ledger* of Philadelphia. She was the first woman to head a major American news bureau overseas. In Berlin, the couple entertained many famous guests including Albert Einstein, Sigmund Freud, and the well-known writer H. G. Wells, author of *War of the Worlds*. She based many of her feature stories on these guests and on others whom she met socially at parties.

Because she was always enthusiastic about finding and writing a story, she scooped many journalists who were less eager.

Joseph did not like living in Berlin, so he spent more and more time in London, without Dorothy. Their lives grew apart, and in 1927, they divorced.

One evening, Dorothy invited several Hungarian government officials and Harry (Hal) Sinclair Lewis, an American author, to celebrate her birthday. This party was the beginning of a long romance. Hal, author of the best-selling novels *Main Street* and *Babbitt*, stayed until three o'clock, long after the other guests had gone. Before he left, he asked Dorothy to marry him.

"Mr. Lewis," she answered, laughing. "I don't even know you!"

"What does that matter?" asked Hal.

For several months, Dorothy spent much of her time with Hal. He was insistent on marriage; she was reluctant. The biggest problem in their relationship was Hal's heavy drinking.

In November 1927, the *New York Evening Post* assigned Dorothy to do a series of twenty long articles. The topic was how the Soviet people were adjusting to life after the Bolshevik Revolution. In Russia, she traipsed up and down the streets with her interpreters, asking everyone she met about their lives, their attitudes toward the new government, and their dreams for the future. She sent fascinating reports back to America.

But, Dorothy was not content. She couldn't get Hal out of her mind, and finally she decided to marry him. "I cannot live by myself, for myself ...," she said. They married in London in the spring of 1928.

After their marriage, Dorothy continued to write. She published her articles on the Soviet Union in a book, *The New Russia*, which received excellent reviews. She wrote and toured the United States on lecture circuits, talking about Russia, Germany, and European politics in general.

A son, Michael, was born to the couple in 1930. Dorothy wrote to a friend that he had "a mighty nose, a quivering nostril, a prodigious frown, a tremendous yell, and a charming grin." Like many well-to-do mothers of that time, Dorothy hired round-the-clock nurses for her baby.

In 1931, Dorothy returned to Germany. She wrote about the growth of the Nazi party, led by Adolph Hitler. The

Saturday Evening Post published more than a dozen of these articles in which she said that the Nazi movement was "the enemy of whatever is sunny, reasonable, pragmatic, common-sense, freedom-loving, life-affirming, form-seeking and conscious of tradition." She interviewed Hitler, a candidate for chancellor of Germany, for an article in *Cosmopolitan* magazine. She wrote about how the Brownshirts, Nazi street thugs, "beat [people], knock their teeth out, break their arms, ... make them kneel and kiss the swastika." Her colleagues in the news offices sometimes heard her sob as she wrote. "If only someone would speak ...!" she pleaded. In 1932, her book on the subject, *I Saw Hitler*, was published.

On August 25, 1934, after Hitler had taken power, an agent from the Gestapo, the Nazi secret police, entered her Berlin hotel room. He told her she had 24 hours to leave the country. She had no choice; Dorothy left.

As she landed in New York, reporters crowded around her. Journalist Dorothy Thompson had scored a first! She was the first American foreign correspondent to be expelled from another country.

Dorothy spent most of the next eighteen months touring the United States to speak against Hitler and the Nazis. She warned that the Nazis would soon threaten the world. "This is my story, this is my song, and this is the only thing in the world that I care about in this moment," she said.

Radio was an essential news source before television became a household item. Dorothy Thompson became a popular radio news commentator.

An editor at the New York *Herald Tribune* asked Dorothy to write a regular column for the paper. "I said I would do it because there are so many things that I care a great deal about," she said. Her 1,000-word column, "On the Record," was an immediate national success with more than seven million readers. Dorothy chose her own topics. They included a wide variety of themes: from the New Deal (an American economic program) to a butterfly collection, to musician Arturo Toscanini. A fellow writer said, "The universe was centered in her sights from the start."

Dorothy was always on the alert for ideas, expressions, and anecdotes to enliven her writing. Sometimes in the middle of a conversation, she would interrupt with "Oh, that's good! Can I have that?"

In April 1937, Hal left her, saying that Dorothy's work had "ruined their marriage." Dorothy and seven-year-old Michael moved into an apartment in New York, where she wrote more than ever. She agonized over the increasing number of Jewish refugees fleeing Nazi Germany, and begged for help for these people. "I say we are all on trial," she wrote. "We who are not Jews must speak ..."

The American State Department agreed, and set up an international Conference on Refugees. "There need be no secret," said the editor of *Foreign Affairs*, "that the State Department's action was stimulated by an article by Dorothy Thompson."

In 1938, Dorothy completed 132 columns, twelve long articles for the *Ladies' Home Journal,* and many speeches and radio broadcasts. She published a book, *Refugees: Anarchy or Organization,* about Jewish refugees. She also bought out two collections of her columns, *Dorothy Thompson's Political Guide* and *Let the Record Speak.*

This incredible output took its toll on Dorothy's health. Her doctors prescribed a variety of pills to help her manage the high stress of her life. But Dorothy had little patience, and admitted it. "Now listen here," she said to a new secretary, "if I speak sharply to you, you're not allowed to cry."

Dorothy flew to England in July, 1941, to cover England's involvement in World War II. She sent many articles back to the United States describing the suffering brought about by the massive bombings by the Germans. She wrote of her admiration for the way the British stood up to Hitler. She had tea with Queen Elizabeth and met with Prime Minister Winston Churchill. She visited bomb shelters, war hospitals, schools, and orphanages. Every visit, tour, and social occasion furnished material for her writing.

In December, 1941, the United States entered World War II. The U. S. became allies with England and other countries in the fight against Germany and Japan.

After living alone for many years, 49-old Dorothy fell in love with Maxim Kopf. Maxim, a Czech who had lived most of his life in Europe, fell just as quickly in love with her. Dorothy warned him, "I think I am an awful woman in any man's life. It takes *so* much understanding." Maxim would not listen to a word of it. "You are the most charming woman I have met in my life," he responded. They married in June 1943.

In her writing, Dorothy criticized the increasing American hostility toward the German people. She wanted Americans to understand that their country was fighting against Germany's leaders, not against individual German citizens. "I do not hold the masses of German people responsible for this war." Some of her articles were published in an exceptionally popular book, *Listen, Hans.*

A young family friend described Dorothy while writing her column: "She'd be sitting up with the secretaries coming in and out, her rather sparse hair screwed up in a pink bandanna and wearing a frilly nightie and old sweater, at least two cigarettes going unnoticed."

During the 1950s, Dorothy spoke on many college campuses and in small towns. She seemed to have two personalities. When speaking in New York, she wore fashionable suits or designer gowns, her silver hair carefully styled. But, while at her farm in Vermont, she wore overalls, and "decorated" her hair with a faded neckerchief.

In 1955 and 1956, Dorothy toured Europe and the Middle East. She wrote articles from the Soviet Union, Turkey, Greece, Lebanon, Iran, Iraq, and Israel. In Greece, she dined with the king and queen.

Dorothy reviewed some of her career in *The Courage To Be Happy* in 1957. "Nineteen fifty-seven concludes twenty years during which I have contributed every month an essay to *The Ladies' Home Journal*—240 in all, and the whole collection equal to six good-sized books! During the same period I was also writing three columns a week for fifty weeks of the year."

But Dorothy had developed a drinking problem, and her health suffered. In 1957, she had surgery for abdominal problems. After colon surgery, she did not recover her energy. She and her secretary hardly managed to keep up with the fan mail which kept arriving.

In July of that year, Dorothy had a heart attack. She had to take medication, and complained, "everything you take to slow up your heart action, and keep down your blood pressure also slows up your mental processes."

Dorothy battled depression. She said that her brain was operating "like a stuck phonograph record" and that she was "drowning in drugs."

Dorothy flew to Lisbon, Portugal to visit her grandsons, and died there, from another heart attack, on January 30, 1961.

She had chosen the words for her epitaph: *Dorothy Thompson Kopf—Writer.*

DOROTHY THOMPSON'S BOOKS:

The New Russia

I Saw Hitler!

Refugees

Dorothy Thompson's Political Guide

Let The Record Speak

Listen, Hans!

Once On Christmas

The Courage To Be Happy

Margaret Bourke-White (Library of Congress)

Margaret Bourke-White, photo-journalist, wrote: "There is nothing else like the exhilaration of a new story boiling up. To me, this is food and drink..."

MARGARET BOURKE-WHITE— PHOTOJOURNALIST

1905 - 1971

Young Maggie White said she wanted to do "all the things that women never do." She thought that being a herpetologist, an expert on snakes, might be the perfect career.

Margaret's father, Joseph White, often took his three children on nature walks. He helped Margaret build cages for some of the snakes she brought home. Other "treasures" roamed freely in the house—caterpillars on the window sills, turtles under the piano, and a tame puff adder who liked to sit on laps.

A curious child, Margaret was also fascinated by industrial machines. Her father once took her to a foundry where metals were melted and cast into molds. She watched, entranced by the brilliant flowing metal and the flashing sparks. She wrote later in her autobiography, "this memory was so vivid and so alive that it shaped the whole course of my life."

Her father also introduced her to photography. Lights, shadows, and shapes came to life for her as she helped him develop negatives. Shutter speeds and lens magnifications were topics of everyday family conversation.

Margaret's mother Lena was a perfectionist. She and Joseph expected their three children to do their absolute best at everything they tried. They were forbidden to do "frivolous" things like reading comics, going to the movies, and chewing gum.

Margaret found a way around the ban on chewing gum. She and her sister hid their half-chewed gum on telephone polls on the way home from school. The next morning, they picked it off, ready to chew again. Margaret liked another aspect of the walk to school. She loved heights, and she walked almost all the way on the narrow tops of fences.

One summer, Margaret raised 200 caterpillars under overturned glasses on the windowsills. She fed them a fresh leaf daily. A few times, the whole family sat all night to catch that magical transformation from a cocoon into a butterfly. When Margaret wanted attention at school, she wore her puff adder wound around her arm.

Margaret did exceptionally well in her studies. In her sophomore year, she won a writing contest. Her prize was three books of her choice. She chose one each on moths, frogs, and reptiles.

In 1921, seventeen-year-old Margaret enrolled in Columbia University in New York City. She planned to major in herpetology. In her second term, she studied photography as well as the required science courses. In the summer, she used her new skills as a photographer at a camp where she worked as a counselor. Her first earnings as a photographer came when she sold snapshots of campers to their parents.

Photography still took second place to herpetology for Margaret. Because the University of Michigan at Ann Arbor offered strong science courses, she transferred there. But photography continued to play an important part in her life. She explored taking pictures with a thin cloth over the camera lens. She liked the blurry, sometimes abstract, look this method created.

While in Ann Arbor, Margaret fell in love with Everett Chapman ('Chappie'), an engineering student. They had many interests in common, including photography. Both of them sold some of their work to school newspapers, and they put on an art show together.

They married in June, 1924, just before Margaret's twentieth birthday. Margaret continued her college courses, and Chappie taught at Purdue University in Indiana. Margaret soon learned that she could not be a perfect wife, no matter how much she tried. After two years of marriage, the couple separated. Margaret vowed never to believe she needed another person as she thought she had needed Chappie. Margaret then changed her name, and hyphenated her mother's maiden name of Bourke with her own maiden name of White.

In 1926, Margaret Bourke-White enrolled at Cornell University in Ithaca, New York, to complete credits for graduation. To earn money, she took pictures of school buildings and grounds as she had at Michigan. *Cornell*

Alumni News used many of her photos for their covers. She made good money selling photos of campus scenes for Christmas cards. Encouraged by her success, Margaret showed her photos of buildings to architects in the area. They assured her that she could find work with any architectural firm in the country.

After graduation from Cornell, Margaret decided to set up her own photography studio in Cleveland, Ohio. She was intrigued with the photo possibilities in the industrial "Flats," an area she described as: "a photographic paradise. The smokestacks ringing the horizon were the giants of an unexplored world ..." The idea of taking industrial photos captivated her. But there was no market for such work. She planned to earn her living with architectural photos and to indulge in industrial photos as a hobby.

She opened the Bourke-White Studio, which she described as "a name on a letterhead and a stack of developing trays in the kitchen sink." The studio also included a "reception room" which became her bedroom when she opened a folding cot there at night.

Margaret's first paying job was to photograph a new school building. To arrange the most flattering shot, Margaret placed many bouquets of asters in strategic spots around the foundation of the school. She placed the camera low and shot up through the flowers. The success of this ingenious photo brought her many more jobs.

Soon, Margaret found the time and money to experiment with photos of the "Flats." She described her thrill as she took shots of the yards at Otis Steel mill early one morning: "Suddenly the mist was warmed with flame as a line of slag thimbles shot out of the dark and, like a chain of blazing beads, rolled over the tracks to the edge of an embankment, below where I stood. Car after car, they tipped their burning, bleeding loads down the slope ..."

Margaret's industrial photography hobby became a job. A bank hired her to take a cover photo of the "Flats" for their monthly magazine.

In 1928, Margaret asked the president of the Otis Steel Mills to let her take pictures inside the factories. Her outside photos convinced him to allow Margaret into the mills. Alfred Bemis, a clerk in a photography supplies store, agreed to help her. Night after night, they prowled on catwalks, teetered on ladders hanging over molten steel, and stretched out on cranes. Bemis later described Margaret on one of her first visits to a mill:

We were standing up high someplace and
they pulled a furnace, and you were as delighted as a kid with a Fourth of July fire-
cracker ...You grabbed your camera and
were off to a flying start ... You had on some
kind of flimsy skirt and high-heeled slippers.
And there you were dancing on the edge of
the fiery crater in your velvet slippers, taking
pictures like blazes and singing for joy.

Using magnesium flares for light, she snapped photos of
liquid steel bubbling in its ladles, the orange smoke which
rose from the molten metal, and trails of flying sparks.

Developing the negatives was almost as creative as
taking the shots. As she worked with developing chemicals,
enlargers, and different kinds of paper, Margaret learned
that her hands had "become an extension of the lens that
took the picture ..." The president of Otis Steel bought 16
of these photos for a booklet, *The Story of Steel*.

In the spring of 1929, Margaret received a telegram:

Have just seen your steel photographs. Can
you come to New York within week at our
expense?

Henry R. Luce

Henry R. Luce was the owner of *Time* magazine, and a powerful man in the field of journalism. Margaret was in New York within a week. Mr. Luce told her that he planned to publish a new magazine, *Fortune*, about the modern industrial world. Margaret eagerly accepted an assignment as photographer. She and her friends joked that if the magazine failed, she would be called Miss Fortune.

For eight months before the first issue came out, she and a writer explored stories together. They recorded a glassmaker making electric light bulbs, an orchid grower tending his test tube flowers, workers in a watch factory, and bank clerks.

Up to this point, Margaret had worked only with single photos. Now she learned how to integrate her pictures with each other and with text.

Margaret chose the Chrysler Building, a New York skyscraper, as a subject. Despite the chill of winter, she positioned herself 800 feet above the street, crouching on a tower that swayed in the wind. She said that welders gave her essential advice: "when you are working at 800 feet above the ground, make believe that you are eight feet up and relax, take it easy."

Margaret's photos brought her wide acclaim. People

immediately noticed her distinctive style—precision, movement, and drama. Unlike many photojournalists of her day, Margaret was not content with a small hand-held camera. She demanded sharp and detailed images that could only be produced using special types of cameras, tripods, and other equipment. Margaret was a perfectionist.

Because she did not make enough money from her photojournalism, Margaret accepted advertising assignments. Some, like Goodyear Tire, required actors and props. In that ad, she photographed a succession of near-accidents in which people were saved because the Goodyear tires worked so well.

Both Eastern Airlines and Trans-World Airlines hired Margaret to photograph their airplanes in flight. She strapped herself into a small open-cockpit plane and the pilot flew under, over, and around a passenger plane which was the focus of the ad.

Despite the excitement of some advertising photography, Margaret preferred news assignments. She was delighted when *Fortune* assigned her to take industrial photos in the Soviet Union in 1930. She did not worry that foreign photographers were banned from Russia. "Nothing attracts me like a closed door," declared Margaret. She showed her photos of American industry to Soviet officials, and they granted her a visa. Her photos of Soviet dams, blast furnaces, tractors, and factories were published in *Fortune*, the *New York Times*, and in her book, *Eyes on Russia.*

Fortune assigned her to record the drought of 1934 in the Midwest. She traveled in a tiny two-seater plane. It crashed, "but very gently and only after sundown the last day," Margaret bragged.

Shooting scenes of the devastating drought changed her life goals. She was no longer as interested in patterns, shapes, and arrangements of objects. "Suddenly, it was the people who counted," she wrote.

At age 32, in 1936, Margaret closed her studio for good and became a full-time photojournalist. Her goal was to produce a book of her photos, based "on a great need to know my fellow Americans better." As a partner to write the text, she chose Erskine Caldwell, author of the bestseller *Tobacco Road,* a novel about poor people in the South.

Although she liked his writing, Margaret was not impressed with Caldwell at first. The writer was shy and moody. Margaret said, "This is going to be a colorless and completely impersonal type of man to work with."

Margaret was excited and Caldwell was passive as they loaded the car with cameras, lighting equipment, and tripods. Four days later, the situation changed dramatically. Margaret explained in her autobiography: "Suddenly something very unexpected happened. He fell in love with me."

The couple stopped at hundreds of towns and farms during that summer. Margaret photographed people suffering from poverty, unemployment, and racism. She snapped Begonia, a youngster who went to school only every other day because she shared one coat and pair of shoes with her sister. She took shots of one-room shacks "insulated" with pages from magazines. She watched a lynch mob react in fury when a sheriff stopped a hanging. The result was a book, *You Have Seen Their Faces*, which became a best-seller.

Also, in 1936, she accepted assignments for a brand-new magazine, *Life*. This was to be an inexpensive weekly magazine focusing on news and general interest stories with a heavy emphasis on pictures. Her assignment was to take the photos for the lead story in the first issue.

The subject was Fort Peck Dam in Montana. Margaret first took the cover picture, showing the huge concrete supports. Then she photographed area residents in homes, bars, and back alleys. The result was a human interest story appreciated by over a million buyers of *Life*.

To photograph another human interest story for *Life*, she waded through swirling water during a Louisville, Kentucky flood. She found another type of story in "home industries" in New Jersey. As described in her autobiography, she sneaked past security guards into a rattletrap building, where:

> "...three generations [sat] making lampshades, ceilings and walls dripping with highly combustible paper lampshade parts. Here I did not pause even to reload cameras, but handed them with the exposed films still inside to my helper, who stuffed them out of sight somehow and made his escape..."

Minutes later, the security guards caught up with her. They destroyed the camera she was using. However, many photos were saved, thanks to her speedy helper.

On another assignment for *Life*, Margaret took photos of the ocean, remote villages, and Eskimo encampments in the Arctic Circle. Near the end of the trip, she received a telegram from Erskine Caldwell: "Come home and marry me." Margaret did come home, but not until she had finished the Arctic assignment to her satisfaction. Back in the United States, she said that she married because "a time comes when it is just too troublesome to remain unmarried."

In 1940, she and Caldwell toured the country, writing another book together. The theme of the book was the reaction of Americans who faced the threat of war. They titled the book *Say, Is This the U.S.A.?*

When the Germans bombed Moscow in July, 1941, the couple were there on assignment for *Life*. Soviet officials banned photography of the destruction, so Margaret and Erskine learned to be devious. At the first sound of the air-raid siren, they hid so that the wardens would not take them to the shelters. After the wardens left, the couple set up cameras and tripods to shoot pictures from their balcony. One especially famous shot was of the Kremlin, headquarters of Soviet officials, lit by sparks from exploding bombs.

As she worked on the book *Shooting the Russian War*, Margaret provided more text than in her other books. She no longer relied on Caldwell to do all the writing. To keep her words and ideas fresh, she transcribed radio shows in which she was interviewed about her trip. "They preserved a certain flavor in the choice of words which was invaluable later when I was writing." Still, she insisted, "I am at the core a photographer."

Sadly, Margaret and Caldwell divorced. She wrote, "I was relieved when it was all over, and glad we parted with a mutual affection and respect."

The United States entered World War II in late 1941. By the spring of 1942, Margaret was the first female war correspondent in the country. As a certified military correspondent, she wore an Army green uniform of shirt and skirt or slacks with gold insignia.

In England, Margaret asked to accompany soldiers on a bombing mission. She was told that only male photographers could go. In her autobiography, she wrote, "The pain of leaving pictures undone which my magazine needed went very deep."

She traveled by convoy toward the North African coast. Her ship was torpedoed, and Margaret's first thoughts were to take pictures. However, as water poured into the damaged ship, she thought only about survival. After a terrifying night in a small lifeboat, she and other survivors were rescued by a British ship.

After that incident, an air force general told her that she could go on a bombing mission if she still wanted to. She had proved that she could face enemy fire without panicking.

Margaret flew over the Sahara Desert wearing electrically heated mittens to keep her hands from freezing at altitudes of 15,000 feet and higher. Flying in the lead plane of the squadron, she took dozens of pictures of falling bombs and of the damage they caused.

Six months later, Margaret was in Italy, photographing the ground war. She called this "the caterpillar view." She photographed Italians living in caves to escape almost continuous bombing. She took shots at a field hospital where medical personnel worked with flashlights and wore protective helmets against falling bombs.

Margaret spent most of 1944 writing a book, *They Called It "Purple Heart Valley,"* about the war in Italy. The book was a success, and Margaret gave much of the credit to her writing. "Much as I love cameras, they can't do everything," she said.

In 1945, Margaret accompanied General George Patton's Sixth Army as they advanced into Germany. At Nazi concentration camps, she took photos of the mass graves. People asked how she could bear to look at such atrocities. "I have to work with a veil over my mind," she answered.

She expressed both agony and hope in a book urging the end of Nazism, *Dear Fatherland, Rest Quietly.*

Between photography assignments for *Life*, Margaret wrote, often for days at a time. She produced journals, lecture notes, and notebooks full of ideas for future stories.

After the war, she spent two years in India, and took photos and notes of common people struggling to keep pace with changing times and ideas. The result was another book, titled *Halfway to Freedom.*

In 1949, Margaret traveled to South Africa. She took photos of raids where police terrorized black men, women, and children with guns and clubs. She photographed black children forced to work under agonizing conditions. To get photos of workers in gold mines, she dressed like a miner, in an oilskin suit and a white helmet. She stepped into a huge bucket, and a pulley system took her down into the shaft, 2000 feet below the surface.

In 1952, she journeyed to Korea, a country in east central Asia where Americans had joined a bloody conflict between North and South Korea. She spent months in small Korean villages. She traveled by jeep, stretching out her bedroll in any available dry space. American soldier-escorts learned that when she said "just one more" photo, they were in for a long wait. One of her favorite shots was of a mother and son. The mother believed that her soldier son had been killed. Margaret photographed their tearful reunion.

In the mid—1950s, Margaret discovered that she had Parkinson's disease, a neurological disorder which causes palsy and paralysis. She could no longer use her typewriter, and often could not load her cameras. Her last photo essay appeared in *Life* in 1957. She spent the next eight years working on her autobiography, *Portrait of Myself.*

Margaret Bourke-White died in 1971, at the age of 67.

MARGARET BOURKE-WHITE'S BOOKS:

Eyes on Russia

You Have Seen Their Faces, with Erskine Caldwell

North of the Danube, with Erskine Caldwell

Say, Is This the U.S.A.?

Shooting the Russian War

They Called It "Purple Heart Valley"

"Dear Fatherland, Rest Quietly"

Halfway to Freedom: A Study of the New India

A Report on the American Jesuits, with John LaFarge

Portrait of Myself

Alice Dunnigan (New York Public Library)

Alice Dunnigan said of her career: "It is a giant step from that ramshackle, unpainted one-room schoolhouse tucked away in the edge of a scrubby, unsightly thicket at Mount Pisgah to the great magnificent mansion known as the White House."

ALICE DUNNIGAN— WHITE HOUSE CORRESPONDENT

1906 - 1983

Because she was female and black, Alice Dunnigan learned early about prejudice.

Every time she tried to play with her older brother Richard, he yelled for their mother. "Make this little old gal let us alone."

Her mother always had the same answer for her. "Alice, why don't you let them alone and go back to your mudpies and dolls?"

Everywhere, she met prejudice because of her color. Blacks were not allowed to go to white schools, had to sit in the backs of busses, were restricted in jobs, and could not enter many stores, restaurants, and libraries.

Alice was born on a farm in Kentucky in 1906. Her father, Willie Allison, paid part of his tobacco crop as rent for their three-room shack. Alice helped her father feed the chickens and hogs, gathered wood chips for the kitchen stove, and worked in the tobacco and corn fields. She also helped her mother, Lena Allison, a laundress. She hung out clothes in all kinds of weather, and mended and ironed shirts for white businessmen.

Alice was an excellent student, and she loved school. Her parents encouraged her to do well in her classes. Her mother was proud of Alice's good marks. Lena Dunnigan was ashamed of her poor education: "About all I learned was how to write my name. I'm an awful poor reader. I wish I could read good," she told her children.

Alice was shy. She hardly ever raised her hand to ask a question or volunteer an answer. Classmates called her Raggedy Ann, because she was overweight and wore hand-me-down clothes. The one light in her life was Miss Arletta

Vaughn, a caring and sensitive teacher. "I'll be a school-teacher when I grow up, just like Miss Arletta," Alice promised herself.

A love of writing inspired her to overcome her shyness when she was thirteen years old. One of the few black newspapers in her area was the *Owensboro Enterprise*. She persuaded them to hire her as a hometown correspondent. Her column consisted of one- or two-sentence notices about a birth, a wedding, or other social event. She received no pay, but Alice was grateful for the praise from editors and readers who liked her work.

She began to think about becoming a journalist instead of a teacher. But she knew this was hardly likely. No white paper would hire a black journalist, and few black news-papers existed. The *Owensboro Enterprise* hired only a few reporters. Still, Alice made a new vow: "I'll write for a newspaper and let people know what other people are doing." She wrote later, "Once you smell printer's ink, you can never forget."

The Dunnigans could not afford the cost of cafeteria meals for Alice while she was a student. She carried a tin bucket to school with cold biscuits spread with fat meat or jam. The smell of hot school lunches with onions and spices tempted her. She decided to earn the money to buy them, and accomplished this by taking in washing.

Every Sunday, Alice filled the laundry kettle from the nearby pond. She stacked wood under it, ready to be lit on Monday afternoon. After school on Monday, she picked up the laundry, scrubbed the pieces on a scrub board, and packed them in a tub of clean water. On Tuesday before school, she rinsed and starched them. Then she hung them out to dry. After school on Tuesday and Wednesday, she ironed them. She delivered the clean clothes on her way to school Friday morning.

After ten years of school, Alice graduated as valedictorian. She did not dare mention that she had dreams of becoming a journalist. She had heard all her life the Negro saying about educated black women: "Either you make a schoolteacher or you end up in the white folks' kitchen." She told her parents she wanted to go to Kentucky Normal School, a college for teachers.

"Why do you want to be a teacher?" her father asked. "None of my folks ever made a teacher, why should you?"

Alice believed she had to accept life as a laundress/cleaner/farm helper. Few grants and scholarships were available for needy students. Black youngsters could not expect to receive any help at all.

Just before the opening of the fall term, Alice's high school principal talked to her parents.

"Send her!" he insisted. "If you get to the place that you don't have the necessary money, let me know and I'll lend it to you."

Happily, Alice boarded the train for Louisville, just in time to meet her first classes. Before she had been at the school 24 hours, she had a job washing dishes and serving in the college dining room.

In June, 1924, she received her elementary teaching degree. Immediately, she applied for jobs in many different counties. Most superintendents did not answer her letters. A few met with her, but told her she needed experience. After one interview, she wrote: "I left the office with tears in my eyes, a pain in the heart, a crimp in my spirit, and a puzzling question in mind on how a young teacher could get experience if she is never given a chance to work."

She almost lost her first real job because the Dunnigan family had no phone. Just one day before the opening of school, a neighbor relayed the message that Alice had been accepted as a teacher at Mount Pisgah, Kentucky.

The next day, 18-year-old Alice began her teaching career at the one-room country school thirty miles from her home. The ramshackle frame building had a rusty tin roof and only two small windows. Yellowing cardboard substituted for the missing panes of glass. A potbelly stove dominated the center of the room. Discarded church pews furnished seats for the 45 students, ranging from grade one to grade eight.

With lots of organization and scheduling, Alice soon found the key to classroom management. Parents and youngsters both appreciated her enthusiasm.

Alice and Walter Dickinson, the church organist, were attracted to each other. Just one year after Alice started teaching, they were secretly married.

The marriage quickly became a burden to both husband and wife. Walter wanted Alice to stay home to help with farm work. Alice had other goals. She enrolled in West Kentucky College to fulfill requirements to keep her teaching certificate valid. Because she wanted to keep other job possibilities open, she also studied typing and shorthand.

She had not forgotten the thrill of writing. She wrote a short story which was published in the town's black newspaper, *The Lighthouse*. The editor was impressed with Alice's skill and invited her to help with layout and proofreading—without pay. This experience reminded Alice of her early vow to write for a newspaper some day.

Alice and Walter grew further apart in goals and attitudes, and were divorced in 1930. Alice then took a job teaching at an elementary school in New Hope, Kentucky.

Once again, Alice fell in love, and once again, she kept her marriage a secret from her parents. In December, 1931, she married a childhood friend, Charles Dunnigan.

Alice became pregnant, and was not allowed to teach school when her condition became apparent. Charles worked at a mental hospital where he was on call 24 hours a day. Lonesome and confused, Alice moved back in with her parents. A son, Robert William Dunnigan, was born in December, 1932. A few months later, Charles walked out on the family, saying that he could not support them.

Alice could not support herself and little Bobby on her teacher's pay alone. Black teachers made about half the salary of white teachers. One summer vacation, she had four jobs. She washed gravestones in a cemetery, worked in a dairy, and also did laundry and house-cleaning.

Alice became interested in, and wrote about, small town politics. She also gave speeches and lectures on the subject. Audiences liked her forceful way of speaking, and political leaders praised her for the way she put her ideas across.

The editor of the *Reporter*, a Louisville newspaper, asked Alice to write a column. She submitted copies of her speeches for this unpaid work. In a second column, "The Achievements of the Kentucky Negro," she highlighted successful blacks in that state.

In 1935, Alice took a job at the *Louisville Leader* office as editor of the women's page, proofreader, and general worker. The next year she enrolled at Tennessee A & I State University to take courses in journalism. With this advanced training, she accepted free-lance assignments for the *Louisville Defender.*

The United States entered World War II in 1941. As American men were called into military service, more civilian jobs became available for women. Alice took advantage of the situation to make a career change; she became a clerk at the Labor Department in Washington, D.C. Her job was not particularly challenging, but she loved living in the nation's capital.

Through her contacts in Washington, she became a part-time reporter for the ANP, the Associated Negro Press. This syndicate served 112 newspapers throughout the country, with a focus on news of particular interest to blacks.

Because she belonged to many organizations, Alice received invitations to fashion shows, debutante balls, award ceremonies, and other social affairs. Readers welcomed her announcements and reviews of these activities. She quickly earned a reputation for writing about society with skill and flair.

When the regular reporter left, Alice became Chief of the Washington Bureau of the Associated Negro Press. Her first assignment, in January, 1947, was to cover a Senate hearing on the possible impeachment of a Mississippi senator. The most difficult part of this assignment was gaining admission to the Capitol Press Gallery in the Senate. Guards turned her away. No black woman had entered that gallery before. Alice persisted. She finally convinced the Senate Rules Committee that she had as much right to be there as the other reporters. She was the first black woman to receive accreditation as a White House correspondent.

Alice wished to delve deeper into government affairs. With White House correspondent credentials in hand, she applied for press credentials from the State Department. She became the first black woman to receive that validation.

Alice Dunnigan's beat covered news from the White House and other government departments, legislative news from the Capitol, judicial news from the Supreme Court and lower courts, and news of foreign affairs from the Department of State.

Sometimes Alice was overwhelmed with the contrast between her new life and her early years. In her autobiography, she wrote of being on tour with President Harry Truman. She was riding in one of the limousines that preceded the President's car. As she relaxed in the luxurious leather seat, memories of her childhood in Kentucky rushed over her. She thought about her family's weather-beaten cabin, and could almost feel the cold winter wind whistling through the cracks. Later, on her way to a luxurious banquet, she recalled the childhood meals of field peas and skim milk.

Near the end of the 15-day trip, a reporter from the Indianapolis *Recorder* snapped a photo that Alice treasured forever. It showed Alice shaking hands with the President under the headline: "President Truman congratulating ANP newswoman, Alice A. Dunnigan, for her contribution to the success of his 9,000 mile tour."

During the Truman Administration, civil rights had become increasingly important, and the federal government issued new regulations against racial segregation. Truman's attempts to undercut segregation, such as his executive order of 1948 that integrated the U. S. Armed Forces, stiffened the determination of some whites to resist change. But these rulings also gave some blacks the courage to fight for their own rights. Alice covered riots, demonstrations, and meetings focusing on integration.

She found racial prejudice everywhere—in hotels, public transportation, group meetings, and in the streets. But, when insulted because of her race, Alice quietly walked away from the situation, preferring dignity to confrontation.

Her son Bob joined the Marine Corps in 1953 after graduation from Kentucky State College. With their child now completely independent, Alice and Charles decided to end their 20-year marriage of separation.

One day, Alice was worrying aloud about her finances. A friend asked, "If you're such a hot reporter as you think you are, why don't you write and sell some magazine articles?" Alice accepted that challenge. Within a few years, she was a contributor to many magazines including *Foreign Service Journal, National Republic*, and *McCall's*. In 1955, she applied for and was granted membership in the previously all-white Women's National Press Club.

Alice continually sought ideas for news stories. She discovered many small items she called "news tidbits." These items were not hard news, but were both exciting and important. These included a story about a Negro doorman who captured a gun-carrying demonstrator in the Capitol. Another story focused on the son of a white father and a black mother who protested his assignment to an all-black Army unit. Such stories became a column, "Washington Observation," for the ANP.

Writing this column led to another assignment. The editor of the Pittsburgh *Courier*, the nation's largest black newspaper, asked Alice to write a column, "Washington Inside Out." She could choose her own topics. "I like the stuff you dig up in Washington," the editor said. "You go to the right places and see the right people."

Alice attended almost every press conference available to her. She rarely missed an opportunity to question the President, cabinet officers, and other officials about their concern for the rights of black people. She described herself as a "flea in the collar" of those who practiced discrimination. She did not allow officials to ignore her.

In 1956, President Dwight Eisenhower was embarrassed by some of her questions. He asked Alice to submit her questions to a government aide before she asked them at a press conference. Alice agreed. But after just one session with the aide, Alice changed her mind. She asked why she, and no other White House correspondent, should be singled out in this way. She refused to participate in this censorship.

The result was that Eisenhower stopped calling on her at press conferences. As *Jet* reported in 1957: "The biggest behind-the-scenes hassle at the White House concerns the alleged refusal of President Eisenhower to recognize ANP's Alice Dunnigan at press conferences. Alice, the most regular attendant... hasn't gotten a word in edgewise in over a year ..."

In 1961, the next president, John F. Kennedy, called on Alice at a conference. She asked a question about alleged voting discrimination. Kennedy answered forthrightly, with no attempt to hide the problem. The ban against Alice was over.

The ANP extended Alice's assignments to include crime, religion, sports and entertainment. Alice was not sure that she was qualified to write on all these topics. However, she accepted the assignments because she believed that a black voice should be heard in all aspects of American life.

In many cases, she felt discriminated against because of

her color or her sex, and often because of both. One baseball player ended a pre-game interview with "I know we are going to lose this game. A woman sashaying around the dugout will surely put the jinx on us."

In her autobiography, *A Black Woman's Experience: From School House to White House*, Alice described her many assignments to cover embassy receptions:

> "Alert reporters had to be able to detect serious conversations, listen well, interpret correctly, and report factually and accurately what they 'accidentally' overheard, without revealing the source... The reporters also attempted to write on the "lighter" social side—the beauty and glamor of the affair, the decoration, the menu, who was there and what they were wearing ..."

In the Kennedy/Johnson administration, she was appointed as education consultant on the President's Committee for Equal Employment.

When John F. Kennedy was assassinated, Vice-President Johnson became President. Alice worked on his Youth Council, a federal organization dedicated to service to young people. She wrote speeches for organization leaders, as well as newspaper and magazine articles reporting on the work of the Council.

In 1970, Alice Dunnigan retired. In her autobiography, she explained that she wanted to be at home "where I can sit back and leisurely reflect on a life well spent ..."

Alice died of an abdominal disease in 1983. She left this summary of her life and work:

> "I feel that one of my most significant ac-
> complishments was the leading role played
> in the demands for equal opportunities for
> black reporters in the nation's Capital... "

ALICE DUNNIGAN'S BOOKS:

A Black Woman's Experience - from Schoolhouse to White House.

The Fascinating Story of Black Kentuckians: Their Heritage and History.

Ann Landers (Library of Congress)

A teenager asked if she should go to a dance with a "creep," the only boy who invited her. Ann Landers answered that she should accept, hinting that she might meet someone who was not a "creep" there.

ANN LANDERS—
ADVICE COLUMNIST
1918 -

On July 4, 1918, the baby who became Ann Landers was born to Abraham and Rebecca Friednman. The baby's identical twin, who became Abigail Van Buren, arrived 17 minutes later. The proud parents named the first child Esther Pauline ("Eppie"). The second twin was Pauline Esther ("Popo").

Their father Abraham owned a grocery store in Sioux City, Iowa. Their mother Becky was content to be wife, homemaker, and mother to her four daughters and one son. The Friednman parents taught their children that hard work and determination lead to success.

Eppie and Popo both had big blue eyes and short dark hair. They dressed alike, and were put into the same classes at elementary school, where they were encouraged to share the same toys and friends. When Eppie, the less musical of the twins, did not practice her violin, Popo would take both lessons.

Unlike many teenagers, Eppie and Popo enjoyed being the center of attention. They were beautiful girls, with slim figures, large eyes, olive complexions, soft black hair, and a confident posture and walk. They were popular and dated frequently. They played up their twin sister role by always double-dating. Next to Eppie's photo in the 1936 high school yearbook it says "Always with Popo." Popo's inscription says, "Always with Eppie."

They took the same courses in high school, a general curriculum which included typing and bookkeeping. Both girls were accepted into the freshman class at Morningside College in Sioux City. From the day they registered for classes, the sisters showed that they were different from the other 800 students. The two Jewish girls on the mostly Methodist campus arrived in flashy coats of skunk fur with black and white stripes.

Eppie and Popo signed up for the same courses, including one in journalism. They also created a gossip column for the weekly school newspaper. No student was safe from being spied on by one of the twins. Those who were "caught" found themselves written up in the column, usually identified only by an initial, with provocative details about where and when he or she had been seen "pitching a little woo." The twins worked hard, and the column was a great success.

In her junior year, Popo announced her engagement to Mort Phillips. Although not engaged at the time, Eppie immediately decided that the girls should have a double wedding ceremony. That winter, after a short courtship, Eppie announced her engagement to Lewis Dryer, a law student.

While shopping for a bridal veil, Eppie was waited on by salesclerk Jules Lederer. It was no coincidence that Lederer, a bachelor, waited on Eppie. A matchmaker cousin, who was not happy with Eppie's engagement to Dryer, had told Lederer that the beautiful and charming Eppie would be in the store soon. The cousin had a perfect eye for match-making. Eppie and Jules were engaged just a few weeks after Eppie sent her engagement ring back to Dryer, just in time to have her groom's name changed on the wedding announcements.

On July 2, 1939, Eppie and Popo married Jules and Mort in a lavish wedding ceremony. The brides wore dazzling white, full-skirted gowns and tiny hats embroidered with pearls. Two hundred guests, and 28 members of the wedding party, watched while the rabbi performed the ritual twice—once for each couple. The twins even enjoyed a double honeymoon trip.

Eppie didn't return to finish her senior year at college. She decided to create a home for Jules, who was pursuing a career in retailing. The following spring, baby Margo arrived.

When the Japanese attacked the United States at Pearl Harbor in 1941, and the United States entered the Second World War, Eppie became a nurse's aide at a local naval hospital . Working in the hospital, Eppie learned a lot about how to listen, and to respond, to people who hurt both physically and emotionally.

Later, the Lederer family moved to Eau Claire, Wisconsin, when Jules accepted an executive position there. Eppie was active in the National Council of Christians and Jews, and worked on many of their charitable projects. Again, she volunteered to do hospital work. She said later, "It was at Luther Hospital [that] I received my basic training in relating to people. Sometimes I just listened to the agonized, fearful, anxiety-ridden patients ..."

Eppie was enthusiastic about volunteering. Americans were struggling with adjustment to a post-war world of returning servicemen. Family members struggled to relate to each other again after absences and tragedies caused by the war. Eppie wrote an article challenging citizens to participate in volunteer work. She badgered a local newspaper editor until he published the editorial. She soon became a popular speaker on the subject of volunteerism. Audiences loved her mix of common sense, humor, and hard-hitting talk.

But Eppie needed more than a child and volunteer work to keep her active mind satisfied. She soon discovered a new outlet for her gregarious personality in politics.

In 1948, incumbent Harry Truman, who had become President when Franklin Roosevelt died in 1945, was running for the office against Republican Thomas Dewey. The popularity polls indicated that Truman's chances of victory looked slim, but he campaigned tirelessly. His hard work and continual optimism impressed Eppie, who decided to work for him on the local level. She organized meetings, wrote campaign literature, and encouraged people to donate money to the campaign. She also took part in many radio and newspaper interviews, and became known for her effective writing, both of handouts and of speeches. She soon realized that she had a talent for leadership.

The hard work of Truman and his campaign staff paid off, and he was elected President. Eppie was also rewarded for her efforts when she was elected chairman of the Eau Claire Democratic Party.

When Jules took a job in Chicago, and the family moved, Eppie lost her political contacts. She kept busy decorating their Chicago apartment elegantly, but was soon bored. Margo was busy most of the day in her private school, and Jules was consumed with his new job. Furthermore, the Cook County Democratic party leaders were not interested in her political skills.

Then one morning, Eppie had an idea. Maybe Ann Landers, the newspaper columnist who gave advice to readers who wrote in to her, needed help. Eppie believed that her experience in volunteer work and in politics prepared her to help with the column. She was not bothered by the fact that she had never written professionally for a newspaper.

When she pursued the idea, Eppie was surprised to learn that the writer who was called Ann Landers had died several months previously. Many women were already competing for the assignment. She took a contest application, rented a typewriter, and set to work.

Each applicant for the position had to answer forty sample letters from readers. The letters covered a wide variety of topics, including interfaith marriage and psychosomatic illness. Eppie worked hard, determined to succeed by the use of her writing skills and personal experiences. She also called a number of well-known experts, whom she quoted in her articles.

Eppie got the job. She was the new Ann Landers. When she arrived at the newspaper's offices for her first day, Eppie found her desk, located in the back of a large office in the city room of the *Sun-Times*, covered with thousands of unopened letters, waiting for her advice.

Eppie Friednman Lederer had become Ann Landers, syndicated columnist for the *Sun-Times* and a dozen other newspapers. Her first column appeared on October 16, 1955. Eppie began to learn firsthand about the agonizing burdens people faced all over the country. She realized that she could not let herself become depressed and over-whelmed with all the misery contained in the daily letters. Instead, she had to rely on the belief in love and compassion that she had learned from her family.

She eagerly accepted advice and help on writing from Larry Fanning, an editor at the *Sun-Times*. At first, she revised each column four or five times before she showed it to Fanning, but soon she gained confidence in her writing abilities.

Eppie could not handle the mail by herself, at least at first. She had a ready solution—Popo could help. Popo had experience with the gossip column in college. Without telling Fanning, or her other bosses, Eppie and Popo began working together on the column. First they worked together in Chicago. After Popo returned to her home in California, Eppie sent work to her there.

This arrangement worked well for a couple of months, until Fanning found out and angrily pointed out that Eppie had no right to share readers' letters with anyone. The collaboration ceased immediately.

But Eppie now had the confidence she needed to do the job, and vowed to send a response to every letter, by mail if not through the column. She requested, and received, a staff of three assistants to help her carry out this vow.

In January 1956, less than three months after Eppie's first column was published, Popo's own column appeared in the *San Francisco Chronicle*. The column was titled "Dear Abby," and Popo wrote under the name of Abigail Van Buren.

Because they both realized that this competition could lead to tension between them, Eppie and Popo made an agreement not to sell their columns in the same cities. However, rivalry between the sisters, and their followers, quickly developed. The agreement to not sell their column in the same territory was soon forgotten. Many readers became staunch defenders of one of the columns, and harsh critics of the other.

To promote her column, Eppie began giving speeches. She talked to teens on subjects like petting, smoking, and drinking alcohol. She also spoke to church groups and civic organizations about life as revealed to her by her readers.

She was a popular speaker, and soon travelled all over the country. People often asked her how she knew what advice to give, and she was quick to say, "I'm not an authority on anything, but I tap the best brains in the country."

Letters poured in from doctors, teenagers, alcoholics, and others from all walks of life. Eppie instructed her staff to sift through the mail. They then gave her the letters they thought would make the best material for her column. She continued to write all the answers that appeared in the papers. Her staff answered the others.

Eppie always gave forthright advice. A wife complained that her husband did Spanish dances using his false teeth as castanets. Eppie answered that the wife should let the husband have fun. When a self-pitying reader wrote, Eppie told her to stop her crying because crying was a waste of time. Another advice seeker wrote that her 60-year-old widowed father had recently married a woman the age of his children. She asked how to keep peace in the family. Ann answered that she should follow the instructions on jars of salad dressing: "Keep cool, but don't freeze."

On the serious side, Eppie soon realized that many people in trouble simply did not know where to turn. She printed the names and addresses of free services, such as legal aid and health counseling, in her columns.

In 1959, Eppie was increasingly concerned about the Cold War, the tension and hostility between the United States and the Soviet Union. After a brief study of the Russian language, she spent several weeks in the Soviet Union. There she conducted a series of in-depth interviews about Russian daily life. Eppie recorded interviews on street corners, attended a court session, visited in homes, and listened to people. Wherever she went, she always had a pencil in her hand, ready to take notes. Eppie had all the best instincts of a reporter. She expressed her impression of the visit in the words of a Russian whom she interviewed: "The Russians are your friends." Her interviews became a popular twelve-article series, which ran in almost 100 American newspapers.

Both Eppie and Jules were working very hard, and she realized their relationship was suffering. They decided to buy a secluded camp in Michigan, thinking it would be a perfect place for the family to spend time together. But Eppie and Jules usually arrived at the cabin with a briefcase full of work. They eventually sold the property.

Readers were always eager for information from Eppie.

In addition to her column, she wrote pamphlets on topics of particular concern to readers. One pamphlet, written for teenagers and entitled, "Necking and Petting and How Far To Go," particularly embarassed her daugther Margo.

Eppie had to become a businesswoman as well as columnist. She accepted paid invitations to speak, and also sought out editors and publishers and persuaded them to place her column in choice spots in their papers. In 1959, Eppie received over 1,000 invitations to speak, and made over 100 personal appearances in 37 different cities. She was also often a popular guest on local talk radio shows.

During the 1960s, Eppie changed her views on some issues. She still stood against interfaith marriages, premarital sex, and divorce. But there was a difference. "I am more compassionate now," she explained. "[I used to think] If I could do it, why couldn't they? It never occurred to me that I had many things going for me other people didn't have, things I wasn't even responsible for ... tremendous energy ... good health." She continued, "the world has gotten racier, and I feel I must respond to what is going on out there. If I'm going to be useful, I'm going to have to deal with all kinds of human problems."

Eppie became chairman of the Christmas Seal Campaign. She worked for the National Council on Alcoholism. She also tried to make more time to be with Jules, and to visit Margo and her new husband and baby.

Over the years the rivalry between Eppie and Popo had grown more intense. Eppie took responsibility for trying to settle the rivalry. At her request, the sisters met in 1964 to discuss past misunderstandings. They agreed to stop personal bickering, but their professional rivalry had become too powerful to overcome.

In 1965, her tenth year as columnist for the *Sun-Times*, the paper congratulated her lavishly, gave her the rights (which they formerly owned) to the name of Ann Landers, and printed a bold advertisement that declared: "We love Eppie so much we all want to tell her we hope she'll stick around for at least 100 more years."

Eppie became increasingly concerned about the American involvement in the war in Vietnam. North and South Vietnamese soldiers battled for control of the country, and American soldiers had been sent there to reinforce South Vietnamese troops. In 1967, Eppie traveled 10,000 miles to tour hospitals in the war zone outside Saigon, the capital of South Vietnam. She spent ten days there, visiting wounded soldiers, joking with them, and thanking them for their service to their country. She took down the names and phone numbers of nearly 100 men, promising to call their loved ones when she got back to the United States. Back at the *Sun-Times*, she wrote two articles describing her visit and her impressions of Vietnam. On learning details of her conversations with soldiers, the *Sun-Times* called her the "Miracle Worker."

Margo and her husband were divorced in 1970s. "I stayed completely out of it," Eppie said later. She had never been fond of Margo's husband, and could sympathize with her daughter's decision. The experience forced her to rethink her opposition to divorce.

During the 1970s, Eppie had more requests for speaking engagements than she could handle. She charged as much as $10,000 for a thirty-minute speech, and the money kept the Lederers living in their accustomed high style even after Jules lost his well-paid executive's job. Eppie bought a 14-room apartment in Chicago's ritziest section. She decorated it ornately with statues, Louis XV sofas, paintings by Dali and Renoir, Chinese vases and marble bathroom fixtures.

Eppie traveled to China in 1974. She spent three weeks there studying acupuncture, sexual customs, divorce, religion, and medical practices. She reported on her visit in syndicated articles.

That same year, 1974, Jules told Eppie that he was in love with another woman, and wanted a divorce. Eppie had suggested in her column that spouses considering a divorce should seek professional counseling, and try a trial separation, before ending the marriage. She never explained why in her own marriage this advice was not followed.

In July 1975, Eppie announced her divorce in her column: "The lady with all the answers does not know the answers to this one," she told her 65 million readers. She also declared that she would never again comment either on her marriage or her divorce.

Many wondered if her divorce would weaken her credibility. Not at all! Readers said it was easier than ever to relate to Ann Landers. She had proven that she was more than an Answer Machine, that her life also had troubled periods. She was a flesh and blood human who loved and lost just as they did. Eppie received more than 30,000 letters about the divorce. Most of them supported her.

How did she feel about changing her mind regarding divorce? "Anyone who doesn't change their ideas over a period of years is either pickled in alcohol or embedded in wood," she wrote.

Eppie also found time to continue her interest in politics. She wrote to President Richard Nixon, asking him to stop the war in Vietnam. She participated in a march for non-violent desegregation in Boston, Massachusetts, and accepted an appointment to a House of Representatives committee studying health issues.

In 1978, *The World Almanac* named Eppie the "most influential woman in America."

In 1982, Eppie supported Ground Zero, an organization dedicated to stopping nuclear proliferation. She published a letter from a reader who expressed fear about a potential nuclear war. Eppie urged her readers to write to the White House, and 100,000 readers did so. President Ronald Reagan responded in her column. He suggested that readers write to Soviet President Leonid Brezhnev instead of to him. Eppie arranged to have copies of her column delivered to President Brezhnev.

In 1986, Eppie made news with a column about unfit medical practitioners. She also wrote, and spoke, in favor of school lunch programs, child care, and the Head Start program.

When asked why she has given so much of her life to helping others, Eppie says, "Givers get the most." At her grandson's ninth-grade graduation, she gave youngsters the advice which she has lived by: "It is not what happens to you that counts, but how you handle it."

Continuing to work hard, Eppie has completed a 1,200-page book of advice and information, *The Ann Landers Encyclopedia from A to Z.* "I'm proud of it," she said. It was "the work of a lifetime." Soon after publication, the encyclopedia was a best-seller.

ANN LANDERS' BOOKS:

Since You Asked Me

Ann Landers Talks to Teenagers about Sex

Truth Is Stranger

Ann Landers Speaks Out

The Ann Landers Encyclopedia

Marguerite Higgins (Library of Congress)

Maggie Higgins hung onto the swinging cargo ropes with all her strength. Sliding down the side of the U. S. army transport, she groped with her feet for the barge waiting below. When she and 38 Marines had dropped onto the deck, they headed for the sea wall at Inchon, South Korea. Maggie crouched in the barge, shielding her precious typewriter from mortar fire, tracer bullets, machine gun bullets, and grenades.

MARGUERITE HIGGINS— WAR CORRESPONDENT

1920-1963

Marguerite "Maggie" Higgins was born in Hong Kong in 1920. Her father was an American working for a steamship company, and her mother was French. Maggie learned Chinese from her nanny in Hong Kong, and French from people she met on trips to her mother's homeland.

When the Higgins family moved to California in the late

1920s, Maggie learned to accept being different. To the neighborhood children, she was a foreigner with a strange accent, a youngster who did not know the neighborhood games and songs. In high school in the mid 1930s, a classmate said, "... she knew she was not like the rest of us. She took herself seriously." Maggie had to take herself seriously. A report card with less than straight A's might lose her the scholarship she needed to attend the private girls' school. She didn't mind studying, as many students did. Maggie was curious, and asking questions was an excellent way to learn. "Some day I'm going to know about everything," she said.

In 1937, Maggie entered the University of California at Berkeley. In her first year, she joined the staff of the university paper. As with every paper, some stories are more interesting than others. Fellow students soon learned that Maggie would snatch the most important assignments from any list of suggestions.

Maggie graduated with honors in 1941, and, always independent, traveled to New York City with only seven dollars and a suitcase. She gave herself a year to land a newspaper job. If she failed, she would return to California to teach French.

But Maggie did not expect to fail. She pushed her way into the *Herald Tribune* by following a group of reporters who were entering their offices. She walked right up to the city editor and asked for a job. He told her there might be an opening in a month or two, because many reporters were being drafted to fight in World War II.

Maggie decided to wait out the time as a student in the Columbia School of Journalism. Almost a year later, one of Maggie's fellow students told her that he was leaving his job as Columbia University correspondent with the *Herald Tribune*. He told Maggie that he had recommended her as his replacement. But, he added, that recommendation wouldn't mean anything. Editors would not hire women as reporters. "Everybody knew" about women: they belonged in the home; they were not bright enough to be reporters; they were too emotional to hold a job; they could not command the respect of those they interviewed. So her friend believed.

Immediately, Maggie put on her best green suit and rushed to the *Herald Tribune* office.

"I know you said you didn't want to hire a woman reporter. But I had to try. I know I could do a good job for you," she told an editor.

After a moment of stunned silence, he answered, "Do you think you could start today?"

Maggie began with the kind of assignment that reporters hate: writing an exciting story about the weather. New York City was experiencing a typical midsummer heat wave. Maggie turned in a wonderful story about a South American jaguar in a city zoo. The animal suffered so from the heat that fire trucks had to come and hose it down. Maggie completed the story with a photo of the fierce jaguar with an ice pack bandaged onto its head.

Maggie continued to report stories the other reporters had missed. One was an interview with James Petrillo, the head of the musician's union, who consistently refused to talk with reporters. Maggie knocked at his hotel room door one morning. Apparently Petrillo thought it was the maid, so he opened the door, and Maggie barged in. In just a few minutes, she charmed him into giving her a story.

She was determined to report on a private meeting with Madame Chiang Kai-shek, wife of the President of China, and a group of U.S. governors. It took Maggie forty minutes to convince the Secret Service to allow her to attend the meeting. Another exclusive!

Two months before she was 22, Maggie married Stanley Moore, a college philosophy teacher. The wedding took place after Stanley received his draft notice, and he left for military service in World War II almost immediately. As a serviceman, he traveled a lot, and as a correspondent, Maggie did the same.

Maggie wanted to go overseas. As she told her bosses in 1944, she was exceptionally well-qualified. She spoke fluent French, had studied German in college, and was at that time studying Russian and Spanish. Besides, she said, she was an excellent reporter and writer.

No, she was told, women were not sent overseas. Maggie knew the arguments by heart. Women were too emotional, not bright enough, not strong enough, and not accepted as professionals. Or so it was believed.

But Maggie would not give up. She took her request to the wife of the owner of the *Tribune*. A short time later, she was assigned to London, and her career took a new turn. Instead of being assigned to write specific stories, she was told to write about "international affairs, part of the war ..." She could let her curiosity take over, and report on almost any topic she thought interesting and important.

From London, Maggie sent articles about how the British were suffering through the bombing by the Germans. She also had interviews with Winston Churchill and King George VI. But she wanted to get closer to the battle fronts. She requested, sweet-talked, and argued. She wrote later, "As a foreign correspondent, my biggest disadvantage [was] being both young and a woman."

Finally, however, she received military clearance to join other correspondents in Paris. There she entered the Hotel Scribe where war correspondents were housed. She stood out clearly as a newcomer in her freshly laundered olive drab outfit. Experienced war correspondents swarmed around the lobby in various stages of battle dress. The room overflowed with helmets, mud-caked typewriters, and bedrolls. Maggie felt just as different as she had when she arrived in her California neighborhood as an eight-year-old immigrant.

Immediately, she made her plans to be the best reporter of all. "I became a cyclone of energy," she wrote in her autobiography. "Each day I read every single French paper ... then I would assign myself to check the validity of every major news development." She requested interviews with French officials and many American military officers, and visited embassies searching for news sources.

Maggie wrote about the living conditions of the French who had suffered through more than five years of war. She also attended American General Dwight Eisenhower's daily press conferences. She also wrote about a near-invitation to dinner with Eisenhower. She had been told she would be invited, but the invitation was rescinded. The next day, a general associated with Eisenhower told her that someone on Eisenhower's staff had vetoed the invitation saying, "I'd never trust those baby blue eyes."

Daily, Maggie sent back about 3,000 words to New York. Each time she filed, she hoped that at least one of her stories would be on the front page.

In March, 1945, Maggie received an assignment to report on the bombed areas inside Germany. She rode in an American Air Force plane, a two-motored C-47, that had to wend its way through bomb craters on the landing strip. In Darmstadt, Munich, and Frankfurt, she wrote of starving civilians, and wounded and crippled soldiers.

Nazis had tortured and killed more than six million Jews in concentration camps. Maggie arrived at Buchenwald, one of the largest camps, a few days after Allies liberated the prisoners there. She wrote about the scene: "Bodies had spilled out of trucks and carts ... trickles of blood and yellow bubbles of mucus oozed from the eyes and noses of the many who had been .... tortured to death." She sent back detailed interviews with survivors who told of unspeakable cruelty on the part of the guards.

Next, Maggie headed for the concentration camp at Dachau. She traveled in a jeep with a reporter for the Army newspaper *Stars and Stripes*. Just outside the camp, Maggie jumped out of the jeep to investigate. She wrote of the incident in *News Is a Singular Thing*:

> "...a watchtower crammed with twenty-two
> SS men [Nazi police]. They were staring
> intently at me. Rifles were at the ready and
> the machine gun was trained on me. God
> knows what prompted me ... I addressed
> myself to the SS guards. 'Come here, please.
> We are Americans.' "

Maggie spoke in German. To her surprise, the SS men surrendered, and Maggie and the sergeant freed the starving prisoners.

For her reporting about Dachau, Maggie received an army campaign ribbon. She also earned the New York Newspaper Women's Club award as the best foreign correspondent in 1945.

After the war was over, Maggie remained in Germany and Austria. She sent home feature stories about the beauty of the Austrian countryside. She also wrote about unusual people: an opera composer; the wife of a Nazi known for his cruelty; a former Russian princess; the butler of Adolph Hitler, leader of the Nazi party.

Maggie did not take her success for granted. "Partly because I am a naturally slow writer and partly because of the fear of making an error, it used to take me longer than most correspondents to accomplish the same thing. So in order to compete, I just had to stick at it longer." However, the star reporter was not so dedicated to making her marriage work. Maggie and Stanley Moore had grown apart emotionally, and were divorced.

In 1946, Maggie traveled frequently to countries behind the Iron Curtain, a symbolic barrier between Soviet-dominated countries and Western Europe. She was arrested once by Polish authorities, and once by the Russians. Soviet agents searched her house, and her secretary was kidnapped by Communist police. One morning at five o'clock, Czech police broke into her room, demanding her passport and other official papers. They had to leave when they could find nothing out of order.

In 1947, 26-year-old Maggie was appointed Chief of the New York *Herald Tribune's* Berlin bureau. She wrote, "It would be untrue to say that I hadn't hoped for the appointment ... but it was unexpected. For I was wearing a chip on my shoulder about the unlikelihood of my paper's picking a female to run an established newspaper bureau."

Maggie's feeling of success was mixed with her overwhelming desire to be best. "I felt that I was coming of age as a foreign correspondent—if only I could hold down the job properly and meet the competition."

Maggie would not let anything get in the way of a good story. She had invited fourteen guests to a dinner party on the night that the Soviets walked out of the Allied Control Council, creating instant chaos among Western leaders. Maggie excused herself to her guests, urging them to go on with the dinner while she wrote the story. Four hours later, at midnight, Maggie returned to the living room, her story completed. Her guests had waited for her; they all finished dinner together at two o'clock that morning.

Once, Maggie was caught in a riot in Berlin. She was thrown to the ground, her arms and legs lacerated by jagged brick and glass. Because she already had a skin rash, the lacerations became ugly, infected welts. Maggie had to spend some time in a Swiss hospital. There, she received news that her editors were going to transfer her because they felt that she was overtired. She immediately left the hospital and rushed back to Berlin to prove that she was feeling fine.

In the spring of 1950, *Herald Tribune* editors transferred Maggie to Tokyo, Japan, against her wishes. To her amazement, however, that assignment turned out to be even more exciting than her previous one. Japan was close to Korea, where North Korean Communists were fighting for control of South Korea. United States and United Nations troops joined the South in battle; Soviet and Chinese troops aided the North.

A *Time* correspondent warned Maggie, "Korea is no place for a woman." One of Maggie's friends agreed, but added, "It's okay for *her.*" Maggie said, "I could not let the fact that I was a woman jeopardize my newspaper's coverage of the war."

In Seoul, the capital of South Korea, Maggie became a refugee when the Chinese invaded that city. She hitched a ride in an American jeep, taking nothing except her typewriter and a few clothes.

She lived with the troops for three weeks. On the battle

field, she was easily spotted in her tennis shoes, baggy pants, and oversized fatigue cap. Like the soldiers, she lived without privacy and with a frightening lack of sanitation. From a foxhole, she wrote about flaming mortars and bazooka patrols. She crawled through rice paddies, reporting the stories of common soldiers. Maggie wrote in her story for the *Tribune*: "There is very little that is not wasteful and dismal about war."

"First-rate war coverage," she wrote in *News Is a Singular Thing*, "requires only two qualities that are not normally demanded of any first-rate reporter ... a capacity for unusual physical endurance and the willingness to take unusual personal risk." One of her companions reported, "She was a good man under fire."

Suddenly, Maggie received orders to leave Korea immediately. The order came from Lieutenant General Walton Walker, head of American forces in Korea. "This is not the type of war where women ought to be running around the front lines," he said.

Maggie answered that she was there as a correspondent, not as a woman. The *Herald Tribune* came to her defense. Maggie appealed to General MacArthur, who rescinded the orders.

Maggie took an assignment to accompany a 38-man Marine unit. The soldiers struggled to secure a beachhead off a port at Inchon, South Korea. She received front-page coverage for her story which included:

> "As we lay there...on our bellies...in a rockstrewn dip in the sea wall...a sudden rush of water came into the dip in the wall and we saw a huge Landing Ship Tank rushing at us..."

One American colonel complained only that she omitted some important facts in her reporting, about her own daring and bravery: "... completely disregarding her own personal safety [she] voluntarily assisted by administering blood plasma to the wounded ..."

In 1951, Maggie was awarded the Pulitzer prize for overseas reporting. She was the first woman to win this award for journalism.

That same year, her book, *War in Korea*, was published. In her foreword, Maggie described the book: "... I have tried to show how the enemy struck, how we fought back, and what we have learned about our weaknesses, our strength, and our future."

Maggie was well-known and respected, both in the field

of journalism and around the country as a whole. She received requests for more than 2,000 speaking engagements in just one month.

Maggie went on a ten-week, round-the-world tour for the *Herald Tribune*. She sent back interviews of important political leaders: Franco of Spain, Tito of Yugoslavia, Nehru of India, the Shah of Iran, and others.

In 1952, 31-year-old Maggie fell in love with and married a somewhat older military man, General William Hall, whom she had known for years. She wrote: " ... I had an exciting professional career. Now ... I had ... something far rarer: a love both true and deep." But Maggie did not let her marriage interrupt her career. She admitted, "My home is where my typewriter is."

In the fall of 1953, the couple's baby, Sharon Lee, was born two months early. Sadly, the infant died less than a week later. Maggie compared the baby's struggle with death to that of wounded solders on the battlefield: "None struggled harder than Sharon," she said.

On a trip to the Soviet Union in 1954, Maggie traveled more than 135,000 miles, interviewing a great many people. Her book about the trip, *Red Plush and Black Bread*, was welcomed by millions of Americans who wanted to learn more about the daily lives of Soviet citizens. Maggie followed this in 1955, with a book about her life, *News Is a Singular Thing*.

When Maggie was eight months into her next pregnancy, she covered a meeting of Soviet Premier Khrushchev and U.S. Vice President Richard Nixon. A month later, she gave birth to Larry, a healthy baby boy. A few months later, she was in Africa, writing stories about problems there.

Maggie signed a contract with *Newsday* to write three columns a week. What a relief after the pressure of daily assignments! By 1959, Maggie and Bill had two children, three cats, two parakeets, a rabbit, a donkey, and a dog. Most of the pets had free run of the house.

In the next few years, Maggie made ten trips to Vietnam, where American military advisors and troops were fighting in battles. In *Our Vietnam Nightmare*, she criticized the American government for becoming involved in that struggle.

After her last trip to Vietnam, she became violently ill. Her temperature was 105 degrees, and she ached all over. She was rushed to Walter Reed Army Hospital in Washington, D.C.

A few days later, she was scheduled to appear on the *Today* show in New York for an interview about *Our Vietnam Nightmare*. She sneaked out of the hospital, and was taken by taxi, airplane, and wheelchair to the studio. She completed the interview before returning to her sick-bed.

Doctors discovered that Maggie had a rare tropical disease called leishmaniasis. The protozoa from the bite of a sand fly had entered her bloodstream and attacked her liver and spleen.

Maggie knew that she was going to die. Her husband later said, "She even thought about what was going to happen to the pets. 'You take care of Blue Kitty,' she told the cook."

Maggie died on January 3, 1963.

In her obituary, the *New York Times* said that Marguerite Higgins "had brass and she had charm, and she used them to rise to the top of a profession that usually relegates women to the softie beats of cooking, clothes, and society."

MARGUERITE HIGGINS' BOOKS:

War in Korea

News Is a Singular Thing

Red Plush and Black Bread

Our Vietnam Nightmare

Charlayne Hunter-Gault (Library of Congress)

Charlayne Hunter-Gault "could give a crash course to the network anchors... she guides us through the show without dominating it, asserting her authority solely through her poise, intelligence and preparation."

The Nation, *July 1993*

CHARLAYNE HUNTER-GAULT— TV JOURNALIST

1942—

Charlayne Hunter-Gault was born in February, 1942. Charlayne was an unusual name, but it was the best that Charles and Althea Hunter could do when the baby girl appeared. She was supposed to have been a boy, and her name was to have been Charles. Charlayne's mother later explained, "I wanted it to be as close to Charles as possible and yet make it feminine." Charlayne wrote later in her autobiography that she liked the name because it was both strong and feminine to her.

As a black child growing up in the southern state of Georgia in the mid-1900s, Charlayne had to be strong. Blacks were discriminated against in housing, employment, public transportation and facilities, and every other aspect of their lives. Discrimination in education was particularly offensive to Althea Hunter, who had attended an integrated school in Chicago. She knew that Charlayne would be condemned to schools for blacks only where teachers and supplies were inferior to those in white schools.

The Hunters, like all blacks, lived with fear because of racial prejudice. Most white policemen and judges were not interested in the rights of black citizens. The Ku Klux Klan, a white terrorist organization, threatened black would-be voters who sought to exercise their rights as citizens.

Charlayne shared a love of reading with her mother. Althea Hunter often read a book every day. At one time, she taught school even though she did not have a college degree. She was hired by a white school board to teach in a black school. "The white folks didn't care what the black folks got," she explained.

Her father was a chaplain in the army. Charlayne saw little of him in the first few months of her life. Then she and her mother moved to California to be near him. Shortly afterwards, however, he was sent to North Africa.

Charlayne and her mother moved in with her widowed grandmother in Covington, Georgia. Grandma Brown was a reader like her daughter. After she finished her day's work of washing and ironing, she always read three newspapers from front to back.

When Charlayne was five years old, she was as tall and heavy as her friend Betty, who was older. Charlayne wasn't supposed to go to school until she was six. But she was curious about Washington Street School, so she tagged along with Betty one day. Nobody paid any attention to her, so she kept going. She loved the classroom, the books, the gravelly red clay playground, and the boiled pig ears and hot dogs the kids could buy for lunch. At the end of the first term, she received a report card! And at the end of the year, she was promoted to second grade!

Charlayne liked playing in the empty lot the neighbor-hood kids used for a playground, riding her bike, and climbing the large mulberry tree to pick the juicy purple berries. With her special friend Betty, she tried out home-rolled "cigarettes," rolled-up newspaper stuffed with weeds from the backyard. They also tried snuff, tiny wads of tobacco tucked between their bottom lip and their teeth.

They also daydreamed about the future, when Charlayne hoped to be a doctor, and Betty a nurse.

Charlayne was an only child until the first of her brothers arrived when she was eight years old. For company, she read a lot and made up her own stories. She loved comic books, especially stories of Wonder Woman and Nyoka, Jungle Girl. She made her two dolls promise they would not tell her secret name, Charlayne Alberta Ruth Nyoka, Queen of the Jungle and All Places. She also learned Bible verses and stories in Sunday School and went to Daily Vacation Bible School. Charlayne says of her religious teachers: "They taught us to believe in ourselves."

Charlayne amazed her friends with her vocabulary. "I lived in the dictionary," she wrote in her autobiography, *In My Place*, of "always looking for unusual words. ... by calling someone 'an antidisestablishmentarian antediluvian antebellum anus spot,' I got their attention..."

In high school, Charlayne entered into both classes and social life enthusiastically. In her starched dresses and bobby socks, she was a typical teenager of the day. At home, she learned to escape from her two younger brothers into her bedroom where she had a record player and her own telephone.

When Chaplain Hunter was sent to Alaska, Charlayne and her mother and brothers went with him. After a while, the teenager became used to the cold and snow, to the fourteen hours of darkness daily, and to her new classes and teachers. But she was the only black in the school. She sat alone and lonely through dances, during which no boy would ask her to be his partner.

Piano playing and baby sitting took up a lot of Charlayne's time. When spring arrived, Charlayne's mother announced that she wanted to go back to Atlanta. But Charles did not ask to be sent there as well. His many assignments away from home had destroyed the once-strong family relationship. He stayed on in Alaska.

Back in high school in Atlanta, Charlayne did some proofreading for the school newspaper, *The Green Light*. Brenda Starr, the red-haired and blue-eyed comic strip reporter, was Charlayne's idol. She decided to become a journalist. Her English teacher told her gently that only white men were journalists, and said that the character of Brenda Starr was not realistic. Even though she was white, Brenda could not be a journalist because she was a woman. Charlayne was told that teaching was a more appropriate— and attainable—goal for her.

Charlayne listened, but did not really believe what she heard. She was sure about wanting to go on to college, and certainly was not ready to accept a limitation on her career goals.

Determined to become a journalist, Charlayne hunted for a school with a strong journalism department. By now her mother managed a real estate company, so the family did not have to worry about finances. Charlayne could not find a college in Georgia that met her two requirements: it had to have a strong journalism department, and it must accept black students.

She preferred to stay in Georgia, but most Georgia state universities and colleges did not accept blacks. This discrimination occurred despite a 1954 Supreme Court ruling which outlawed segregated public schools. Charlayne did not consider trying to break the discrimination barrier in Georgia. She enrolled at Wayne State College in Detroit, Michigan, where the journalism courses seemed excellent.

However, members of the Atlanta Committee for Cooperative Action did think about breaking the barrier. They wanted two exceptional black students to become a "test case." They asked Charlayne and her classmate Hamilton

("Hamp") Holmes to apply to an all-white state college or university. Charlayne and Hamp agreed to take part in the plan. Charlayne believed she had nothing to lose, because she was already accepted at Wayne State.

Charlayne and Hamp filled out applications at the University of Georgia. As expected, they were rejected. The registrar said that the dormitories were full, so the college was accepting only students who lived in the immediate area of Athens, Georgia.

The NAACP, the National Association for the Advancement of Colored People, immediately applied for a restraining order against the college, accusing its officials of discrimination. The two teenagers assumed that nothing would come of the case. Charlayne completed her plans to go to Wayne State. Hamp registered at Morehouse University, a black college in Atlanta.

At Wayne State, Charlayne was assigned to a two-room suite on the tenth floor of a dormitory. Her roommates were both white. She discovered that only two other black women lived in the dormitories. However, classes were integrated. In the college dining room, students generally separated themselves into black or white groups.

Charlayne was disappointed that she was required to take basic liberal arts courses for her first two years. No journalism until she was a junior!

In the summer of 1960, Charlayne and Hamp were summoned to federal court. Their NAACP lawyers argued that the University of Georgia had discriminated against them. The judge did not agree, but he did not close the case completely. He ordered Hamp and Charlayne to apply again in November.

That summer, Charlayne's friends in Atlanta protested against discrimination. One of their procedures was to insist on service in an all-white restaurant—a sit-in. They persisted until police arrived. Officers arrested them, took them to the station, scolded them, and then let them go. Charlayne wanted to protest with her friends. But her awyer advised her not to get involved. An arrest record might ruin her application to the University of Georgia.

In her second year at Wayne State, Charlayne joined the Delta Sigma Theta Sorority. This group was dedicated to preserving the memories of the struggles of black women, and working against further discrimination. Charlayne said that learning this proud history "was stiffening my backbone and adding yet another coat of armor for what lay ahead." The sorority stood for fun, too. Charlayne and two sorority sisters became a popular singing trio at informal campus parties.

That fall, she was called to Athens for an admission interview at the University of Georgia. She applied for the second term, and then headed back to Wayne State.

The University again rejected her application, saying that she would lose credits if she registered in the middle of the year. At a December trial, NAACP lawyers argued that the university had accepted other (white) transfer students for second term enrollment.

The ruling came on January 6. Charlayne was in Detroit when she heard the news on the radio. The judge ruled that the University of Georgia had discriminated against Charlayne and Hamp, and he ordered that they be admitted to the second term.

Two days later, Charlayne was on her way to the Athens university. National and local newspapers shouted the news of the judge's edict, reporters swarmed all over the city, and protesting white students burned crosses on the campus.

Charlayne was assigned to a room in Center Myers, a University of Georgia dormitory. She was the only student living on the first floor. She went to sleep with the sounds of chanting outside her window: *Two, four, six, eight/ We don't want to integrate.*

On the second night, students threw bricks, sprayed tear gas, and shouted curses. Later, she remembered thinking, "So this is what it feels like to be in the middle of a riot.... As I was unpacking, a brick flew through the window splattering glass all over my new college clothes." State troopers escorted her out of the dormitory that night. They told her that school officials had suspended her from classes. "For her own safety," they had said. Hamp, who had taken a room off-campus, was also suspended.

NAACP lawyers went to court again. The judge ordered the university to re-admit Charlayne and Hamp by 8:00 the next Monday morning. The two students dutifully returned to the campus, and did their best to ignore the protests and demonstrations.

Editors of a black Athens paper, the *Inquirer,* asked Charlayne to write a front page article on her experience. Her report was widely read and discussed.

Because they appreciated her writing, the *Inquirer* next asked her to write about segregation problems at the local high school. Years later, she described her feelings as a fledgling reporter:

"I was a 19-year-old kid, and I was working for a rag-tag newspaper, but I had the guts to call [the superintendent's] office... 'Hello, this is Charlayne Hunter, and I'd like to speak to the school superintendent about these deplorable conditions over at David T. Howard High School.' When she came to the phone, she answered my questions like I was a serious person. I said to myself, 'Man, this is heavy!'"

That summer, Charlayne was an intern at the Louisville *Times*. The position didn't offer much work; interns learned mostly from observing. Charlayne wanted to do more. She volunteered to write two human interest articles, and both were accepted and published.

In the fall term of her senior year, Charlayne offered to work on *The Red and Black*, the University of Georgia newspaper. As a new person on the staff, she worked on making "dummies" and doing other mechanical work. She asked for reporting assignments, but was never chosen. After a while, she realized that she was not chosen because she was black. She soon quit the paper in protest.

Senior year in college was a time for Charlayne to do

some serious thinking about her life. She no longer believed in Brenda Starr. But her desire to become a journalist was much stronger than it had been when she admired that cartoon character. Charlayne had learned about the power of the press as she studied articles about her own experiences at the University of Georgia. She knew that journalism "had the awesome power to help change things." She wanted to share in this power.

During that school year, she fell in love with Walter Stovall, a slender, blond fellow journalism student. They married secretly. Neither wanted to be distracted by the publicity that their marriage would create. They had a daughter, Susan Stovall, before their short marriage ended.

After graduation, Charlayne eagerly accepted an offer to work as an editorial assistant at *The New Yorker*. The sophisticated magazine featured nonfiction articles, as well as short stories and poetry. She worked there for three years, learning about the business of being a writer. Part of her job was to contribute items for the popular "Talk of the Town" column.

In 1967, she received a Russell Sage Fellowship to study social science at Washington University in Missouri. This was the start of a series of exciting moves for her. As part of her study, she went to Washington, D.C. to investigate the Poor People's Campaign, a series of demonstrations against poverty. While there, she visited station WRC-TV. That station hired her as an investigative reporter. She soon became the anchor of their local evening news program.

Charlayne became known for her writing skills, careful research, and social perception. Although the anchor job was exciting, she could not resist an offer to write for the *New York Times*. In 1968, she left Washington to work for this top American newspaper, and stayed for the next ten years. She specialized in stories about Harlem, a major black section of New York City. She also covered a wide variety of news items that affected the black community: in-depth articles about drug addiction, black activist groups, teenage unemployment, and civil rights struggles.

In 1971, she married Ronald Gault, a specialist in public finance.

As Charlayne moved ahead in her career, she questioned herself continually. She told an interviewer: "You have to assess every situation that you're in and have to decide, is this happening because I'm black? Is this happening because I'm a woman? Or is this happening because this is how it happens?"

In 1978, Charlayne received a job offer from the Public Broadcasting System. She was hired as substitute anchor for Robert MacNeil and Jim Lehrer on the nightly *News Hour* show. Besides her appearances as anchor, Charlayne did a lot of writing for the show. Again, she distinguished herself through careful research and thoughtful comment. An executive of *News Hour* said of her: "She has an intense curiosity—coupled with a sensitivity and a humanity."

In 1983, Charlayne became the national correspondent for that show. Although MacNeil and Lehrer had the final say on programming, Charlayne was invited to propose ideas she would like to see investigated on the air. She also contributed ideas to pieces written by other reporters. An example of this occurred during the 1992 Los Angeles riots. Though Charlayne was busy at a conference in the Midwest, she talked with program writers several times a day "making sure that my ideas were included in whatever deliberations went on."

Charlayne worked for over a year to research a television piece on infant mortality among blacks. The story appeared on *News Hour*. Then Charlayne expanded the information to create a documentary on the plight of black teenage mothers.

In 1993, while still a part of the *News Hour* staff, Charlayne became the news anchor for *Rights and Wrongs,* a Public Broadcasting System program. The program, called a "viewsmagazine," reports on human rights abuses throughout the world. An interviewer described Charlayne's work as "framed by journalistic rather than dramatic considerations; instead of being geared to provide a moment's excitement on the screen, they serve to clarify and give both factual and analytical depth to the issue at hand."

Today, Charlayne wants to help young journalists to make the most of their lives and careers. She advises students to take advantage of every possible learning experience:

> "If you live in this country and you want to report in this country, you have to know where everybody in this country came from ...You can't put yourself in the communications business and not know about the rest of the world."

BOOK BY CHARLAYNE HUNTER-GAULT

In My Place

GLOSSARY

anchor: one who narrates and/or coordinates a news show.

exclusive: a news item obtained by only one person or source.

intern: one engaged in supervised practical training.

muckraker: a person who exposes political corruption.

network: a chain of interconnected radio or television stations.

press conference: an opportunity for interviewers to question leaders.

Pulitzer Prize: a prize awarded annually for achievement in journalism, literature, and music.

syndicate: an agency that sells articles for publication in several newspapers or magazines simultaneously.

viewsmagazine: a television news program featuring opinions.

INDEX

SELECTED BIBLIOGRAPHY

ourke-White, Margaret. *Portrait of Myself.* New York: Simon & Schuster, 1963.

Brady, Kathleen. *Ida Tarbell: Portrait of a Muckraker.* New York: Seaview/Putnam, 1984.

Dunnigan, Alice Allison. *A Black Woman's Experience— from Schoolhouse to White House.* Philadelphia: Dorrance Company, 1974.

Goldberg, Vicki. *Margaret Bourke-White.* New York: Harper & Row, Publishers, 1986.

Higgins, Marguerite. *War in Korea.* New York: Doubleday & Co., 1951.

Higgins, Marguerite. *News Is A Singular Thing.* New York: Doubleday & Co., Inc., 1955.

Howard, Margo. *Eppie: the Story of Ann Landers.* NY: G. P. Putnam's Sons, 1982.

Kurth, Peter. *American Casandra.* Boston: Little, Brown, & Co., 1990.

Landers, Ann. *Ann Landers says, Truth Is Stranger....* New Jersey: Prentice-Hall, Inc., 1968.

Liesgor, Peter and Marguerite Higgins. *Overtime in Heaven.* New York: Doubleday & Co., Inc., 1964.

Marzolf, Marion. *Up from the Footnote*. New York: Hastings House, Publishers, 1977.

Mills, Kay. *A Place in the News*. New York: Dodd, Mead & Co., 1988.

O'Neil, Paul. "Twin Lovelorn Advisors Torn Asunder by Success," *Life*, April 7, 1958.

Pottker, Jan and Bob Speziale. *Dear Ann, Dear Abby*. NY: Dodd, Mead & Co., 1987.

Robertson, Nan. *The Girls in the Balcony*. New York: Random House, 1992.

Sanders, Marion. *Dorothy Thompson: A Legend in Her Time*. Boston: Houghton Mifflin Co., 1973.

Schlipp, Madelon and Sharon Murphy. *Great Women of the Press*. Illinois: Southern Illinois University Press, 1983.

Sheean, Vincent. *Dorothy and Red*. Boston: Houghton Mifflin Co., 1963.

Tarbell, Ida. *All in the Day's Work*. New York: The Macmillan Company, 1939.

Tomkins, Mary. *Ida Tarbell*. Boston: Twayne Publishers, 1974.